The Heart of Happiness

13 Techniques Using Mindfulness and Humor to Manage Stress and Find Happiness

CHRISTY EIDSON

Copyright © 2019 Christy Eidson

All rights reserved.

ISBN: 9781098646790

DEDICATION

Thank you to my daughter, Allison. I love you!

CONTENTS

	Acknowledgments	i
1	Introduction	1
2	Stress	5
3	You Are Not Your Circumstances	57
4	Change Your Brain	69
5	What Is Happiness?	93
6	Stress Management Techniques	103
7	Making Your Life Easier	164
8	The Plan	170
9	Take ACTION	192
10	Time Management	211

ACKNOWLEDGMENTS

This book would not have been possible if not for my great grandparents, George and Elsie Eidson, who raised me. They are long gone, but their tough love prepared me for the real world, whether I was ready or not. We did not have a lot, but I knew that they loved me. I am also grateful for the love of my daughter, Allison.

I am so thankful for the support and encouragement of my friends Sissy Debut, Amy Delvin, Ellen and Mark Greenbaum, Jana Mandes, Sandra Dee Nicholson, Carolyn Pachuilo, and Maria Tucker. They all have inspired and motivated me, and I greatly appreciate them all.

I want to thank Vanderbilt University for keeping me alive! If it wasn't for the staff and surgeons, I would not be here to write this book.

And finally, I want to mention Randy Alexander, who is pictured in the book with his dog, Rufus. He always saw the best in people, and his life's mission was to spread happiness and cheer. (Also pictured are my dogs, Roscoe and Freddie.)

1 INTRODUCTION

What if I told you that you could start living a happier, more fulfilling life today? Do you want to sleep better and have more energy? Imagine living life with purpose and meaning.

Many of us are dealing with stress at a chronic level. Because of this constant stress, we are finding ourselves not only physically, but also mentally and emotionally depleted. Stress has become an epidemic and is costing us greatly. It is driving us to the doctor and is even driving us to our graves. Chronic stress is connected to six leading causes of death!

One constant truth with all people is that we all want to be happy. But happiness isn't the same for everyone. We must decide what we value, what our priorities are, and what actually makes us happy. Most of us do not know where to start on that discovery.

Some may ask what do I know about the subject of Happiness? I do not have a doctorate in psychology. I didn't even study psychology other than a couple of classes in college. There are no cool titles or letters before or after my name. No Dr. Eidson or Christy Eidson, Ph.D. I'm just your average Joe. I finally found happiness, but it took a lot of work. I am experiencing the lowest level of stress that I have felt in years.

I am not happy one hundred percent of the time, but I have learned various ways of coping with the negatives when they pop up. I have spent half of my life suffering from depression and anxiety. I have lost jobs because of it, shut people out because of it, and even lost my home because of it. But I have come out on the other side. I have found purpose in my life, started a business that fulfills me, and found joy in the small things. I have learned to stay in the moment and really enjoy the here and now.

I may be a comedian, but this is a serious book. It is a very serious topic and one that we see affecting most of us on a daily basis. It is a perfect topic for a comedian to cover because, as a group, most comedians are affected by anxiety and depression. We use humor as a coping mechanism in dealing with stress in our search for happiness. We search and search for exterior elements to make us happy, but that won't happen, at least not for the long-run. True happiness comes from within.

I have been doing standup for over 15 years. I have been suffering from anxiety and depression for twice as long. I have been suffering from chronic insomnia for the better part of the past decade. It has taken me half of my life of trial and error to figure out what works for me to cope.

There are many books on motivation, anxiety and depression, stress management, and personal transformation. Rarely, do any of them discuss happiness and how to achieve it. This book will help you reduce stress while seeing your life in a new light. In this book, you will be able to define stress and identify stressors, discover helpful and effective stress management techniques that have been proven to work, and develop a plan to reach your goals. This book will also help you realize what happiness means to you. I haven't selected these techniques flippantly. They have worked for me, but why? I started researching the science behind each one and share it with you here.

Similar books may cover one of these topics, but I wanted to create one book that encompasses all of them. I make the material more relatable by using pop culture references to illustrate my points, which makes it easier for people to identify with.

This book is divided into four parts. The first part examines stress and how your personal history affects how you handle stress today. The second part goes into the process of rewiring your brain and defining what happiness is and what it means to you. The third part delves into effective stress management techniques that have been proven to work and is backed with science. And the fourth section goes into goal setting and developing a plan of action.

I wish a book like this had been available twenty years ago when I was going through my deepest depression. But it is available now!

2 STRESS

What is Stress?

"Do not dwell in the past, do not dream of the future, concentrate the mind on the present moment." ~ Buddha

Stress is a normal part of everyday life, but not all stress is bad. Stress is the body's natural defense against danger. Stress can be a motivator to get you off your keister and turn thoughts into actions. Stress was beneficial when we were cavemen, trying to escape predators like the saber-toothed tiger. Moderate stress can bring people together. No one can argue that 9/11 was a stressful event in American history, but it helped to bring us together as a country. We became a community and put aside our differences to help each other. It can create a sense of urgency and that action needs to be taken. In May 2010, Nashville was hit with what was called a "500-year flood". During this time, neighbors banded together to help salvage and rebuild each other's homes. Stress can be positive, but also life-changing, like getting a promotion or giving birth. Stress can be seen as challenging and not a threat. However, if stress is prolonged, it becomes problematic for our health.

Negative stress is when the reaction continues without relief. This can be dangerous.

When a stressful situation arises, our bodies go into a physical and mental response to the stress. This response is referred to as "Fight – Flight – Freeze". Some of these may only be a perceived danger or threat as opposed to a legitimate threat. Regardless, our body releases stress hormones that prepare us to either: fight off a threat, flee from the threat, or freeze like a deer in headlights. When stress becomes long-term, the body can experience things such as hardening of the arteries, weight loss or gain, depression, anxiety, high blood pressure, chest pains, or digestive issues. The emotional aspects of this continued stress can often surface in the form of depression or anxiety.

Stress also becomes dangerous when we use unhealthy coping mechanisms to relieve stress. Abusing substances or engaging in damaging behaviors, such as food, alcohol, drugs, sex, or compulsive shopping or gambling, alleviate the stress momentarily, but eventually, end up compounding the problem by keeping the body in a stressed state.

According to the American Psychological Association, chronic stress is connected to six leading causes of death: heart disease, cancer, lung ailments, accidents, cirrhosis of the liver, and suicide. More than seventy-five percent of all visits to the doctor are for stress-related issues. Our bodies are built to go into fight-flight-freeze whenever we are faced with stresses for survival. But because of our constant exposure to the stresses of modern life, we are in a perpetual state of fight-flight-freeze, which takes its toll on your bodies. Heart disease is the number one killer in the United States with over 600,000 deaths, which equates to roughly one out of four deaths being from heart disease. Suicide is the tenth leading cause of death among adults in the United States, according to the American Foundation for Suicide Prevention.

There are different degrees of stress. Acute stress is typically short-term and the most common. An example of this would be if you were cut off in traffic or had an argument with a co-worker. Once the threat passes, the stress is reduced. It may cause a headache or upset stomach. Episodic acute stress may be experienced by someone who had a lack of organization or is overloaded with commitments. It caused the person to excessively worry and can lead to high blood pressure. Chronic stress is the most harmful. Examples of chronic stress would be stress that the person cannot seem to escape, as in a person with ongoing poverty or in an unhappy marriage. People can become used to the stress and not even really notice the effect that it has on the individual. It becomes part of who the person is. They may even experience a mental or emotional break-down, heart attacks, strokes, or even suicide.

When stressed, the hypothalamus of the brain reacts by sending signals to the adrenal glands, which release hormones. These stress hormones include: cortisol, adrenaline, and norepinephrine. Cortisol is the primary stress hormone. It raises the amount of glucose in the bloodstream, alters the immune system response, and suppresses the digestive and reproductive systems. Adrenaline increases your heart rate and elevates your blood pressure. Norepinephrine is similar to adrenaline, and it allows you to become more aware and focused.

Stressors

In order to know how to manage stress, it is beneficial to be able to identify the stressors. A stressor is anything physical or psychological that causes a stress response.
Here are a few examples:
    Physical Stressors

- Dehydration
- Lack of Sleep
- Overworking

Psychological Stressors
- Bad Habits
- Low Self-esteem
- Lack of Organization
- Procrastination
- Technology
- Debbie Downers

Dehydration

Here's a catch-22: Stress can cause dehydration, and dehydration can cause stress. While the adrenal glands are producing stress hormones, when stress is long-lasting, the adrenals become fatigued. When this happens, the body loses its ability to regulate its fluid levels, which triggers dehydration. During stress, our heartbeat speeds up, and our breathing becomes faster and shallow. If we are being chased by a lion, we may even pee our pants, thus losing more fluids. We sweat more and our mouths get dry, which all lead to dehydration.

Lack of Sleep

You may be completely exhausted, but the moment that you get into bed, your brain just won't shut off. You toss and turn. You try to get comfortable to no avail. Minutes turn into hours, and you just cannot fall asleep. It is frustrating, and most of us have experienced this at some point in our lives. Sleep deprivation is one of the most common stressors. Difficulty sleeping and staying asleep, as well as, the quality of sleep can be affected by stress. Our brains and bodies need to rest. A lack of quality sleep can affect memory, judgment, and mood. Chronic sleep deprivation can contribute to obesity, high blood pressure, heart disease, and accidents, and can lead to anxiety and depression.

The University of Rochester did a study in 2013, in which they found a possible link between sleep and brain disorders including Alzheimer's. When asleep, the brain cells of mice would shrink in size. The brain bathes in cerebral spinal fluid that flushes away toxins in the brain.

Not only is inadequate sleep a problem, but addiction to sleeping pills can also create further health issues, even death. There are countless stories of celebrities who had chronic insomnia to the point of needing sleeping aids to get any sleep. One such well-known example would be Elvis Presley. After performances, he would be so wired from the adrenaline of performing, and his insomnia was so chronic, that he often needed sleeping pills, or downers, to be able to fall asleep. In addition, you will see that celebrities will also need barbiturates, or uppers, to be able to arouse from their slumbers and be able to function. This was an epidemic issue from the 1950s Hollywood to even today. But insomnia is not just prevalent in the celebrity circles; the common individual can fall prey to this vicious cycle as well.

Not only do sleeping aids have the potential to become addictive, but they also lose their potency as the individual builds a tolerance to the medication. Often times, someone will fall victim to an overdose because of this. The respiratory system becomes depressed, and the person, basically, stops breathing. The lack of oxygen to the brain ultimately results in death. We see this all too often in tabloids and on celebrity shows. If you watch celebrity autopsy shows (and I totally do), you may see that there appears to be a link in celebrity deaths and sleeping aids and anti-anxiety medications. Many people who suffer from anxiety and depression also struggle with insomnia.

Overworking

In our modern age, overworking has become a mainstay. The Japanese are facing an occupational hazard called Karoshi, which translated literally means "death by overwork". Employees are committing suicide or suffering from heart failure or stroke due to excessively long work hours. According to an article in Business Insider, more than twenty percent of Japanese employees work an average of 49 hours or longer each week. A woman in Tokyo worked 159 hours of overtime and took only two days off in one month before she died of heart failure in July 2013. In China, 600,000 die each year from overworking. In the United States, 85 percent of men and 66 percent of women work more than 40 hours per week. According to the International Labour Organization, "Americans work 137 more hours per year than Japanese workers, 260 more hours per year than British workers, and 499 more hours per year than French workers."

In some instances, workaholics are replacing one addictive behavior for another. Some alcoholics, for instance, are trading their addiction to booze for more hours on the job. While this behavior is more positive, it is still an addiction nonetheless. With more work comes more stress. The quality of life is often lower with our bodies and lives out of balance due to excessive work schedules. We are drained mentally and physically with little or no time to recuperate.

Bad Habits
Sometimes, you do not think of your habits as being stressful, but they can be. Often times, bad habits are being utilized to combat stress. Activities like eating, smoking, drinking, and drugs are used to mask feelings and alleviate stress, but they only work temporarily. Overeating can lead to obesity, which has its own plethora of health issues, including the potential for heart disease and diabetes. Smoking affects your lungs and can also lead to cancer or heart disease. Excessive drinking or drug usage can

result in health issues as well as legal pitfalls. Excessive shopping and gambling can fritter away money, quite unnecessarily. Also, shopping addiction can lead to disorganization, clutter, and even hoarding, which creates even bigger stress issues. Most of these bad habits also involve spending money to afford these habits, which money is a huge stressor for most. Some people resort to risky sexual behavior to feel a release from stress, but this is only a momentary relief. Such behavior can result in unplanned pregnancies or sexually transmitted diseases.

Low Self-Esteem

When we view ourselves as inadequate or unworthy, we may be suffering from low self-esteem. These beliefs are usually not built on fact, but rather negative thought patterns. When life's obstacles come our way, the person with low self-esteem views these situations as threats instead of challenges to overcome. This raises our levels of stress.

Often times, we put everyone first instead of ourselves. We may ignore our own needs and wants in order to spend time with other people and attend to their needs and wants. We may feel unable to say no as to not let them down or disappoint others. We may do this due to a sense of responsibility or a sense of obligation. This can create a burden on our own well-being. It is okay to say no. If you have ever been on an airplane, the flight attendants tell you that in the event of an emergency, place the oxygen mask on yourself first before you attempt to help others. Why is that? You are no good to anyone else if you have not taken care of yourself. Sometimes, you have to put yourself first!

Low self-esteem can often be traced back to childhood. Maybe a parent, teacher, sibling, or friend said something that stuck with us. It has been said that we need to hear five compliments to cancel out one criticism. However, when you are young, that one negative comment is the one that sticks with you. When we are young, that is the most impressionable time of our lives. Criticisms from those we respect and from those of authority have quite a bit of weight on our psyches.

Whenever we begin this negative self-talk, we need to ask ourselves if these comments are based on facts or not. Most of the time you will come to realize that thoughts like "I'm not good enough" or "No one loves me" is not based on any truth at all. If you really sit and think, you know there were times that you were exceptional at something you did. You know that there are friends and family that really do love you. This negative self-talk creates a vicious cycle of low self-esteem and stress. When these negative thoughts creep into our heads, we have to combat them with positives. Replace negative comments like "No one loves you" with positives ones like "my friends and family love me and are there for me when I need them."

Another way to look at low self-esteem is to ask yourself this: the things that you say or think about yourself, would you say them to someone else? Would you tell someone that you cared about that they weren't worthy or that no one loved them or that they didn't deserve happiness? Probably not, unless you were a total, heartless jerk. If you wouldn't say things like that to someone you love, why would you say them to yourself? To be truly happy, you need to love yourself more than anyone else. And that is not being selfish or conceited. That is being assertive and confident, and it is showing yourself respect.

Social media can be a great way to catch up with friends and keep up with what is going on in the world, but it can also be a dangerous minefield for the self-esteem. Social media can be a platform for bullies and the negative Nancys of the world to spew negativity. We may also feel let down by comparing ourselves to other people. We only see what other people let us see. What we see in our feeds may appear to be the perfect marriage, a great relationship, or a budding career, but in fact, these people may have lives that are not so rosy or may have a darker side that they are not sharing on the World Wide Web. Therefore, we cannot compare ourselves to others. If you are going to compete with anyone, just compete with yourself. Make a goal to be a better person than you were yesterday.

Instead of spending time online with people that you may not even know in real life, spend time with people you actually know and love, and know that they love you in return. Take the time to know how they feel and share with them how you feel. Spending time with those that we care about doing activities that we enjoy making memories that last a lifetime. It also lowers your stress and increases your happiness. Social bonds are crucial for long-term happiness.

Lack of Organization
Disorganization can make us feel helpless or out of control. The chaos can appear to snowball and overwhelm us.

Organizing can be time-consuming. It can also be emotional. Determining whether to eliminate things from your life can be a struggle. Sorting through memorabilia, old clothes, and such can bring up memories of the past, give concern for the future, and make you wonder about where you are right now. Are these objects really a necessity or are they excuses for not moving forward with your life? If you have clothes that you have not worn in six months or more, chances are that you will not miss them. Are you holding on to smaller clothes just in case you lose those fifteen pounds that you haven't lost in the past ten years? You probably won't miss those either. Are you really holding onto these items for practical reasons or psychological ones? If you have ever watched an episode of the TV show *Hoarders*, you will see that these people hold onto their possessions for emotional reasons.

Some people even keep old boxes from a cellphone that they used five years ago…with the cellphone still in it. Okay, that one is me. Am I going to use it again? Probably not. Ditch it! Are you holding on to an old Christmas ornament that you will fix when you buy some glue? It's not going to happen. If something meant a lot to you, you would have made it a priority and fixed it long ago. Obviously, you have it in the junk drawer, because you *might* use it again, but you haven't, and there is a good chance that you won't.

Technology

Technology is possibly the newest and most addictive stressor, currently speaking. For example, the average American watches over five hours of television per day, according to the New York Times. The Entertainment Software Association published a report that surveyed over 4,000 households. It found that 63 percent of U.S. households included at least one frequent gamer, this included PCs, consoles, and smartphones. Online gamers spent 6.5 hours a week on average playing. In 2017, Common Sense Media released a report stating that children up to age 8 spend an average of 2 hours and 19 minutes on screen media each day. Children between the ages of 4 and 12-years-old, the average time spent using screen media was 4 hours and 36 minutes. On average, young people between the ages of 18-25 spent an average of 3 hours and 25 minutes each week just watching someone else play video games online. Yes, these people were not even playing the games themselves; they were watching other people play!

Even keeping up with current events can be a stressor. Much of the news reported is negative. Murder, war, rape, and shootings tend to grab the headlines. "If it bleeds, it leads." And if there is a positive clip, you can be sure that it will end up at the tail end of the newscast, between sports and the anchor sign-off. Is it because we secretly crave negativity, or is it what we have been programmed to look for? We are becoming conditioned to think that the worst is right around the corner and creeping through our neighborhoods.

Negativity

Like stress, we can't avoid the negativity, it seems. Debbie Downers are around every corner. They are the office gossips. They are the keyboard warriors on social media. They are the authors of tabloid magazines. They are the family members who have come down with the newest popular disease trend that they just read an article about. Aunt Jan, it's not Lupus. You have a bunion!

These Negative Nancys can't see the forest for the trees. Instead of seeing the rainbow, all they see are the dark clouds. They could have happiness right within their reach, and they won't ever see it. Those kinds of people are no picnic to hang around and no person that you want to be. Negativity itself becomes a bad habit that we need to break. Some of these Negative Nancys will say that they are being realists. I say that you can be positive and still be a realist. They will continually see problems where none exist. They will create problems where none exists. Of course, things aren't going to be rosy all of the time, but a positive, optimistic outlook makes for a much better coping mechanism. In a world of Eeyores, be a Pooh!

It is nearly impossible to avoid negativity. It is around us everywhere every day. It's on the news, on social media, and even at the dinner table. Even reuniting with an old friend can remind you of the negative qualities that each of you possesses. Maybe he is cynical, and maybe you are easily frustrated by other people's bad habits. Regardless, you have to find methods to navigate through this world of negativity while maintaining your sanity.

Negativity can become a heavy weight that keeps you down and holds you back from attaining your happiness. It is the proverbial albatross around your neck. It is negativity's job to keep you out of focus, to undermine your thoughts and feelings, and to make you lose perspective. It keeps you from moving forward to achieve your goals. Negativity keeps you from getting off the couch and being productive. Negativity tells you that you can't or shouldn't.

But sometimes, these negative devils can become little angels. They may have the gift of pointing you into a direction that you may not have considered. They can sometimes make you think outside of the box. Negatives can be turned into positives, and it all depends on your perspective of the situation.

I had one such devil. There were some local comedy shows around town, and I felt that this one booker kept overlooking me. I finally complained to him about this slight. Instead of acknowledging this oversight and agreeing to book me, he simply replied, "If you don't like the way that I book my shows, why don't you start your own?!" Although his tone was cutting, and he was obviously brushing me off, I looked at this as an opportunity. Instead of bending to his will and accepting my defeat, I decided to use spite to motivate me. This, of course, is not the preferred method of motivation, but for me, it lit a fire under me. I sat down with some other female comedians, whom I felt were also being snubbed, and we discussed starting a female-only show.

So many comedy bookers are appalled at the idea of an all-female line-up, as if that would make it difficult to draw a crowd. My idea was that half of the population is female, and just about any comedy audience is comprised of about half female or more. There is definitely a market. I knew that there was a niche that was not being served. I marketed my show as serving the female and the LGBT market. All the performers were to be female or gay. So in essence, I was filling two available niches. And I was right! The show was a success right out of the gate. I ran the show for over five years until I felt I needed to move on and work on something else.

I could have let this jerk keep me from what I wanted, which was performing. I could have let him win. He had the perceived power, which after all was said and done, was not power at all. He could not control all the rooms and all the stages. I turned this obstacle into an opportunity to find a new venue, create a new show, and ultimately, move the show to the local comedy club and become very successful doing it. He could not say that. I took the power back and created something meaningful and beautiful with it.

Procrastination

Ironically, I put off writing on this stressor last! It plagues most of us at one time or another. We know what we need to do. Why can't we just do it? We make lists, plan schedules, read self-help books, and watch motivation videos, but nothing seems to work. We spend the time that we put aside to complete our tasks by watching TV or surfing the internet. We are stuck to our sofas like gum on the bottom of a shoe. We cannot manage the strength to just get out of bed! We come up with tons of distractions to avoid doing what we need and want to do. We make convenient excuses for delaying our action. We create our own speed bumps and roadblocks. Most of the time, it is all based on fear.

We may try to take steps to help us overcome our procrastination, but to no avail. We may make deadlines for ourselves, but if they are not concrete, they will not work. Then, when we don't stick to them, we beat ourselves up when our goal is not reached or deadline not completed. This sinks us further in our hole of procrastination, because we feel defeated.

Sometimes we put things off until the time is just right. Or sometimes we delay because we don't want to do it unless we do it perfectly. Well, I've got news for you. There is no right time and there is no such thing as perfect! That is not to say that perfectionism cannot work in your favor, but it can only work if you put it into action. Any action is better than no action at all. Remember, the thousand-mile journey starts with one step. The hardest part is just showing up! Don't put it off until tomorrow, because tomorrow never comes. You only have today.

We become so transfixed on the outcome that it prevents us from even starting. We are looking at the process all wrong. It is not the destination that we should focus on, but the journey. We need to be involved in the total course of events. We need to be in the moment. After all, the end result is not what makes you happy, even though we believe that it will. It is the process that leads to happiness.

Anxiety, Depression, and Therapy

I used to work for this computer company, and for legal reasons, I won't say the name of the company, but it rhymes with Hell. I had been hired for technical support. Yes, technical support. I could set the clock on a VCR, but that was about the extent of my technical prowess. At first, it was fun, because we were in a classroom setting and learning new things. I have always done well in classroom settings, so this was good for me. But after the training was over, we were put on the phones. For eight hours a day, I did nothing but answer call after call after call of problems.

I knew that every time my line would ring, it would be someone complaining, crying, yelling, or worse. No "you're doing a good job", no "I love my machine", none of that. Each and every call was a problem. Nothing but negativity eight hours a day, five days a week, that is, unless they imposed mandatory overtime!

Well, as the months drew on, I began getting some stomach problems: nausea, an upset stomach, cramping. The doctor asked me if I could be pregnant. I said, "Not unless it was immaculate conception." It would come and go, but soon began to be more frequent. I went to the doctor thinking that I may have a bug or some sort of ulcer. The doctor ran tests, but in a few weeks when the results came back, they were all negative.

I went back to work, and the symptoms grew and got worse. All that constant negativity was definitely taking a toll on me, mentally and physically. I began sweating a lot, even in the winter. My hands would shake. I would wake up in the mornings, and my body would be stiff, and I couldn't stop shaking. My heart was pounding so loudly that I thought that I could hear it. No matter how deeply I would breathe, it felt like my lungs would not fill up with enough air. My neck muscles would ache from all the tension in them.

So the doctor ran more tests, and again, in a few weeks, they all came back negative. Then, the doctor sat me down and asked me some questions. She had a checklist. It had questions like: how often do you have these symptoms: often, sometimes, rarely, never. Symptoms like: difficulty concentrating, difficulty falling asleep, trembling, twitching, irritability, sweating, dizziness, muscle tension, shortness of breath, heart palpitations, fatigue, nausea, lightheadedness, and on and on. Well, of the twenty-three or so symptoms, I am happy to say that I had nineteen of them. When I do it, I go all the way!

After she reviewed the checklist, she told me that it looked to her like I was suffering from anxiety and panic attacks. She diagnosed me as having generalized anxiety disorder. I honestly did not think that she, the professional, knew what she was talking about. These were very physical, very real symptoms. And you're saying this is all in my head? No way! Then she presented me with the brochures...lots and lots of brochures, and pamphlets, and whatnot. She asked me if there was any history of mental illness in my family. Hmmm....yeah! Any alcoholism or drug dependency in my family...okay, I get it. She said that panic attacks cause very physical symptoms, and that when some people experience a panic attack, they think they are having a heart attack. Pretty scary! Crazy runs in my family. I had a great grandmother that was agoraphobic, a cousin who suffered from post-partum depression, and an aunt that developed dementia and routinely pooped her pants...I suppose that she thought it was funny.

I was going to the bathroom constantly. I was having hot flashes and cold flashes. I was praying that it was extremely early menopause. I couldn't fall asleep, even though I was exhausted with fatigue. My anxiety had gotten so bad that I had trouble even going to the store. I would walk in, and I felt like people were everywhere and they were all standing way too close to me. I felt like people were heavily in my personal space. I felt very hot. The aisles seemed to close in around me. I just had to get out of there. Thank god for food delivery or I would have starved to death!

Soon, I also developed a severe case of depression. For me, the depression was stronger than the anxiety. Instead of freaking out, I just wanted to stay in bed and not move. Then, I began sleeping all the time. I would wake up at 2:00 in the afternoon, and by 5:00 p.m., was back in bed again. I had these waves of fatigue that were so strong, that when I had them, I had to lie down immediately.

The doctor prescribed some medication for me: several types of medications, in fact, over the course of the year. I tried Prozac, Zoloft, and Paxil. They said some of the newer medications had fewer side effects than older antidepressants, but they sometimes produce slight nausea or jitters when people first start to take them and that these symptoms fade with time. Unfortunately, they made my symptoms worse and even gave me symptoms I didn't have before. On Zoloft, I was walking into walls and just generally felt that I was freaking out. Paxil made me sweat like a pig! Disgusting! Then, she tried Xanax. We have a winner! Xanax is generally prescribed for short periods of time, especially for people who have abused drugs or alcohol and who become dependent on medication easily. For that reason, doctors don't like to prescribe them. One exception to this rule is people with panic disorder, who can take them for up to a year without harm.

I also began seeing a therapist. She told me that people with generalized anxiety disorder go through the day filled with exaggerated worry and tension, even though there is little or nothing to provoke it. They anticipate disaster and are overly concerned about health issues, money, family problems, or difficulties at work. Sometimes just the thought of getting through the day produces anxiety. My mind was constantly racing. I was worried about money, about everything. I'm a list maker, so I had tons of little pieces of paper all over the places with lists on them. I was seriously losing it. Sometimes, if I could manage to actually get out of bed, I would drive all the way to work, get to the parking lot, and just could not step out of the car. Needless to say, the job didn't last long. The anxiety was so severe that I felt like I was out of control and just couldn't pull it together.

My therapist started me on a Cognitive-Behavioral Therapy which is very useful in treating anxiety disorders. The cognitive part helps people change the thinking patterns that support their fears, and the behavioral part helps people change the way they react to anxiety-provoking situations.

She said that I needed to get to the root of what was causing this. But I had no clue. She told me that a serious loss, difficult relationship, financial problem, or any stressful change in life patterns can trigger it. Check, check, check, and check. Very often, a combination of genetic, psychological, and environmental factors is involved in the onset of depression and anxiety. Women experience depression about twice as often as men. Many women face not only hormonal stresses, but additional stresses such as responsibilities both at work and home, single parenthood, and caring for children.

During therapy, she began asking me about my family and growing up. She asked me if I was married or in a relationship. I am somewhat of a commitment-phobic. I fear being attached to someone and dependent on someone. This could be due to the whole growing up with a controlling, overprotective parent-figure. I also have a fear of abandonment, which could be due to all the deaths in my family. I have a fear of failure. This could be in part to my realizing that every beginning must have an end, either a breakup, death, or something that causes separation. Why start something if I know it is just going to end? That has been my philosophy on personal relationships for some time now. Negative, I know. I also never wanted to end up in a relationship that was negative, especially one where there were fighting and arguing involved. I had way too much of that growing up. I also never wanted to expose my daughter to that. No child should grow up that way. I also have a fear of success. What if I do get into a good relationship? Will I know what to do? I never had any role models in this area. I didn't know how to make a relationship work.

Fear

"The only thing we have to fear is fear itself." ~ *President Franklin D. Roosevelt*

Fear is our greatest roadblock to achieving our goals and successes. We worry excessively and unnecessarily. We worry about things that we have no control over.

There are only two ways of looking at things: Positively or Negatively. There is no sense in focusing on the things that are detrimental to your happiness. Instead of focusing on what you don't want in your life, you must place your focus on what you do want. Fear keeps us from doing this. That negative self-talk keeps us in a cage. It keeps us from pursuing our fullest potential.

According to Dr. Karl Albrecht, there are five types of fear: extinction, mutilation, loss of autonomy, separation, and ego-death.

Fear of extinction is the fear of ceasing to exist. This goes beyond a basic fear of death. People in this fear category may have fears that include: the dark, heights, or flying.

Mutilation is the fear of losing a body part or losing its natural functionality. These people have phobias with spiders, snake, sharks, or any animal that they believe to be harmful, as well as anxiety involving needles, germs, or even going to the dentist.

Loss of autonomy involves being restricted, confined, trapped, or suffocated. Some label this fear as claustrophobia when it is a physical fear. Otherwise, these fears apply to situations in our lives and relationships. This is a broad fear group which can include: fears of commitment, poverty, illness, or aging. It combines feelings of being overwhelmed, trapped, and restricted.

Separation, often referred to as a fear of abandonment or rejection, deals with one's need to belong, respected, and be connected. These people are triggered by a loss of a friendship, a divorce, the ending of a relationship, or the death of a loved one. Jealousy is a good example of this fear.

Humiliation, also shame or worthlessness, or as Dr. Elbrecht refers to it, is the "ego-death". We all want to feel loved and valued, but when our feeling of worth is diminished, we can feel great despair. This category includes triggers such as: failure, bullying, criticism, mistakes, and even public speaking. If you have ever been caught in a lie, you've felt this.

If you suffer from anxiety or depression, they might stem from fear. Fear is universal. Everyone fears something. One person might have a phobia of spiders. Someone else may have a fear of the dark. Public speaking is the number one fear of most people beating out death! Regardless of the fear, most fear is not based on fact, but on perceived threats. Are most spiders deadly? No. Is there a boogie man out to get you in the dark? Probably not. If you get on a stage to speak before an audience, will you die? I almost did, but that's another story.

Ask yourself, what is the worst thing that could happen? What could be as bad as dying on stage? Pooping your pants maybe? I did that, too. I had the worst case of the flu in my life. It had turned from viral to bacterial or vice versa. The doctor prescribed me an antibiotic, to which I ended up being allergic, and the side effects were vomiting and insane diarrhea. I had a stand-up comedy show in Knoxville, Tennessee, and I was drinking Pepto like it was going out of style. So it was show time, and this was the last night of the run, my tummy was rumbly, to say the least. It was nearing the end of my set, and I felt it happening.

If you have seen the movie *Bridesmaids*, you know the scene that I am referring to. When all the bridesmaids and the bride get sick after eating in a restaurant, the bride was wearing a wedding gown and ends up pooping in the dress in the middle of the street. That was me…kind of. I clenched up like I never clenched before. I crossed my legs while standing, but nothing helped. I tried to power through my last joke, talking as fast as I possibly could. It was too late. I could feel it coming. I didn't even make time to shake the emcee's hand. I ran to the bathroom. Bad news, (I know you're thinking how can it get worse) I had another show after that one! But I did it. If I can live through that and a heart attack, I can do anything. You can, too. Maybe not crapping yourself, but if you can imagine that worst thing that can happen and live through it, you're going to be okay.

Here is a list of some of the most common fears:

- Fear of Disease, Sickness, or Poor Health
- Fear of Loss
- Fear of Dying
- Fear of Abandonment/Loneliness
- Fear of Uncertainty about the Future/Unknown
- Fear of Success
- Fear of Failure
- Fear of Making Decisions
- Fear of Conflict
- Fear of Rejection (including expressing feeling, intimacy, or embarrassment)
- Fear of Inadequacy/Judgment
- Fear of Change
- Fear of Pain (physical or emotional)

Of course, there are many more fears than this, but this is to exhibit that we all share these fears. We all have to find ways to cope with them on a daily basis. The key is to find the source of this fear. Most addictions begin as a way of coping with stress, and most stress has a basis of fear.

Fear of success may sound ridiculous to some, but for many people, it is just as great of a fear as failure is. Fear of failure can keep people from attempting to pursue a goal and is the cause of some people's procrastination. Fear of success can also keep people from attempting to pursue their goal, because if they accomplish their goal, then what next? They must go on and create more goals, bigger goals, and that can be quite scary.

Death is a fear that most people have in common. As I said, it is second only to public speaking. Part of that fear is because of the unknown. We have never experienced it, so we don't know what to expect when it happens or what happens afterward. But if it is something that is inevitable, and there is nothing that we can do about it, then why worry about it? If you have seen the movie *What About Bob* with Bill Murray, he is plagued with fear. He cannot leave his house. He is petrified of taking a bus or touching a doorknob or using a public telephone. It has made him practically immobilized. If it wasn't for his desperate need for a psychiatrist's counseling, some would call him agoraphobic, which is a fear of leaving your home and being in public.

Serious As A Heart Attack

"Life is hard. After all, it kills you." ~ Katharine Hepburn

Death at a Funeral
Some people think about death once in a blue moon, a fleeting thought that floats in and out of the recesses of their minds. Some

never think about it...really think about it. I think about death in some form every single day of my life. I think about when I'm going to die, how I'm going to die, will I be naked when I die? I then I think, of course, I'll be naked when I die. I probably have an unusually thorough concept of my own mortality.

I've been to so many funerals in my life, I've become somewhat of a funeral expert. I've been to so many funerals that most of my wardrobe is black, just to be prepared. I've been to so many funerals that they refer to me as pallbearer number three. I can't hear "the Old Rugged Cross" without tearing up, on cue.

I've developed an anxiety disorder in reaction to death. I went to a lawn and garden show with a friend of mine several years ago. We got to the flower arrangement section, and there were all these big arrangements of beautiful flowers. It was late May, getting ready for June bride festivities, and there were lilies, carnations, roses... all white. When most see a big bunch of white flowers, they would think wedding...not me; I'm thinking funeral. I started to have a panic attack. I got short of breath, jumpy, light headed. I freaked out and dove into the koi pond. I can't go back to the Nashville Convention Center because of that...and a couple of other things, too, but I won't get into all that.

I come from an unconventional, dysfunctional family. When I was little, and still now, people would ask me about my family, and I had my response down. I was raised by my great grandparents, because my mother died when I was five, and I never really knew my father. The first thing out of their mouth was, "great grandparents?" Yes, great grandparents. We pop 'em out quick in the Eidson family. In fact, the women in my family don't bother getting married, so I come from three generations of Eidson women. My mother's maiden name IS my last name. And so was her mother's. We don't like change.

Don't Fear the Reaper

The first Wednesday of the month, I produced a show at the area comedy club. The show was called "Girl On Girl Comedy and Revue", and it featured female and gay comedians, burlesque acts, musicians, and pole dancers. I had been doing this show for a couple of years now and was sitting in the green room, waiting for the show to begin. All of a sudden, I felt very hot and achy. It was June, and I had heard of several people acquiring summer colds. I dismissed how I felt as me possibly coming down with one. It felt like the flu. As I finished my beer, the feeling passed, and I headed to the stage to start the show. The show went on without a hitch. Some of the other comedians and I even went out to a bar after the show and sang karaoke. Everything seemed fine.

The next day, I felt like there was an elephant sitting on my chest. If you have ever had bronchitis, it feels somewhat like that. I was also coughing quite a bit. Both of these symptoms supported my thought that it was a cold or bronchitis. I had decided that if I felt like this the following day that I would go to the doctor. On Friday, I felt fine, so I dismissed it. By Saturday, it was back and to a stronger degree. I was coughing so hard that I thought I may urinate myself. I could not get comfortable. Standing, lying down, or walking gave me no signs of relief. Sunday, I was going downtown to do a tour, and I felt quite disoriented. I felt drunk as I was walking down the sidewalk.

I had been taking medications to alleviate my symptoms. For my cough, I was taking cough syrup. I took Benadryl in case it was allergies. I even took Xanax in case it was just my anxiety flaring up. Nothing helped. I thought that my disorientation and woozy feelings were a result of taking these medications.

At that time of year, we had a music festival going on downtown, and there was a medical tent set up. I thought that I would stop in and ask them some questions. My feeling was that if they expressed concerns, I would go to the emergency room after the tour was over. Once I told the medics that I was experiencing chest tightness, they refused to let me leave the tent. The old "I've got to go tell my boyfriend something real quick" didn't work. They would have been responsible if something happened after I left the tent, they explained. So they put me in an ambulance. They said they would be low key about it, as to not draw attention. Unfortunately, there was a handful of little silver-haired ladies standing nearby, watching me be put on the gurney and into the ambulance. I could just imagine by the looks on their faces that they must have thought I was drunk or hopped up on drugs or something. They didn't put the siren on, but they didn't have to. The extremely loud beeping sound of the ambulance backing up caught everyone's attention! "In case no one is looking, right over here! Look at this person being hauled off."

In the ambulance, they hooked me up to an Electrocardiogram, or EKG, to take a look at my heart. They said it looked normal, but gave me some aspirin to chew up and a nitroglycerin tablet. I immediately felt better. After they moved me into the emergency room, they hooked me up to another EKG. They also took my blood. They checked my blood pressure and said that it was a bit high, but said that they EKG looked okay. The technician said, "You're EKG looks good. We'll wait until your blood work comes back, but we'll probably release you."

By now, I am starving, so I'm planning where I'm going to go after I get out. Should I get steak and a beer? Maybe a little cheesecake for dessert? When the other technician brought in my results, the first technician's face changed. "I did not see this coming," he said. "You're enzymes are elevated. You've had a heart event." Heart event? What does that mean? I asked if he meant that I had a heart attack. He said, "A small one." A small one? That's like saying, "You're kind of pregnant."

He then went on to tell me that they would have to run some more tests. I asked, "Okay, when do I need to come back for that?" He said, "Oh, you're not leaving." I was then admitted. I was floored. How could it be a heart attack? I was only forty years old! Only old people had heart attacks, I thought.

So I got settled into my room, not really sure what to expect. The next day, they wheel me into the ultrasound room. It was just me and the ultrasound technician. He was a very meek, quiet fellow. He was not much for chit-chat, so I tried to break the ice. The only time that I had ever had an ultrasound is when I was pregnant. While he was performing the test, I made the comment, "I think I see the head." I didn't even get a smirk from him, and that was funny! That is when I knew it was serious.

The next test they performed was an arteriogram. During this procedure, the doctor inserts a catheter into an artery in your leg. The nurse came in to shave me before the procedure. What I thought would be my leg ended up being my groin. As she was shaving me, I said, "I think I owe you dinner now." At least, she laughed. After the catheter is inserted, they shoot a dye into your arteries to monitor the flow of blood. This will allow them to see any blockages, as well as revealing any damage or narrowing of the arteries. I will have to say that was the most action that I'd had in a while.

Once that was finished, they wheeled me back into my room to wait for the doctor to review the findings. A few hours later, the doctor entered. He was a handsome, young surgeon, but super serious. "He couldn't possibly be old enough to know what he was talking about," I thought to myself. He introduced himself and began to make a crude drawing on the dry-erase board. He drew a heart and pointed out where I had three blockages: two were ninety-percent and one was eighty percent. Everything that he said after that became very muffled, like Charlie Brown's teacher in Peanuts. He said that I would need to have surgery: a triple bypass. Again, I asked, "When do I need to come back for that?" Oh, I wasn't leaving. Surgery was scheduled for Wednesday. I didn't even have time to worry. I asked him how many times he had done this operation, and he retorted, "About two thousand times." At least, that had made me feel a tad better.

All that I could think about were all of the things that I had put off or had not done yet. But at the same time, I felt helpless to worry. What would worrying accomplish? I would be lying if I said I was not nervous and scared. I was petrified, but at the same time, oddly calm. There was absolutely nothing that I could do about this situation. I had to put all of my faith in this Indian Doogie Howser. This man was clearly well-learned, well-trained, and well-prepared. I had to put my faith in his abilities. I didn't have a choice.

The next morning, as they prepped me for surgery, I had to rely on my humor to stay sane and not breakdown crying. I had a song stuck in my head that oddly gave me strength and serenity: Blue Oyster Cult's 1976 hit "(Don't Fear) The Reaper." "Seasons don't fear the reaper, nor do the wind, the sun or the rain, we can be like they are." There was no sense in fearing what was about to happen. It was out of my control. The song gave me a sense of solace. I found it ironically comical to be singing that song to myself. It was a matter of laugh or cry, or in this case, laugh or die.

As they wheeled me into the holding area, I tried cracking jokes with the orderly. They gave me a lovely blanket made of what looked like bubble-wrap and readied me for anesthesia. The orderly rolled me toward the surgery room, and I was still joking about the situation. I asked him if he ever had patients joke as they were being carted off to surgery, and he said sternly, "No, never." I'm still not sure if that was a good thing or not on my part. I was not in denial; I just saw no need in fighting it. My life was literally in their hands. I had to put my trust in their abilities.

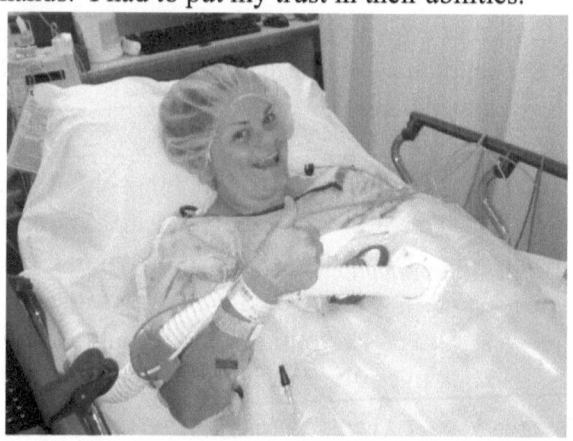

On June 12, 2013, I had a Coronary Artery Bypass Graft, also known as a CABG (pronounced: cabbage). In layman's terms, I had a triple bypass. This is referred to as open heart surgery. That is a very serious surgery that is done to treat people with severe coronary heart disease (CHD). Basically, plaque builds up inside the coronary arteries and can cause heart attacks and even death. The surgery is intended to improve the flow of blood to the heart. During this procedure, the blocked arteries are bypassed with healthy artery or veins that are grafted from other areas like the arm or legs. The surgery takes several hours to perform and the opening of the arteries can last ten years or more.

I woke up several hours later in the recovery room with tubes coming out of me and wires everywhere. The only way that I could communicate was a feeble attempt at sign language with my flailing of the arms. It is hard to convey "Get the fuck away from me!" without using words.

The surgery was a success, because I was still alive, however, I could barely move. Just moving from the bed to a chair seemed like an insurmountable act. Just the thought of coughing or sneezing was excruciating. My chest had literally been split open and sewn together with metal. Pulling the drainage tubes out of me was just as horrible to feel as it is for you to read. Imagine pulling off a band-aid that is inside you, and you will have an idea of what it was like.

Blood vessels from my leg were removed and used to connect to other arteries to bypass damaged arteries. This is called Coronary Bypass Artery Grafting. Nearly 500,000 CABG procedures are performed each year in the United States. It is one of the most common major operations. That did not settle my nerves at all.

Heart disease is the number one killer in the United States, and it accounts for nearly one in every four deaths. It tends to be more prevalent in men than women, but is the leading cause of death in both genders. According to the Center for Disease Control, heart disease is responsible for over 600,000 deaths in the United States each year. That is nearly the current population of my home town, Nashville, Tennessee. The first couple of times that nurses told me that I almost died, I ignored it. Then, a few more nurses and doctors told me that I almost died, I still brushed it off. But after a few dozen people tell you that you almost died, you sit up and take notice. These statistics could have included me!

They had me stay in the hospital for several days for observation and rehabilitation. Needless to say, I was the youngest one in rehab. The other patients were primarily elderly and some with pacemakers, but we were all in the same boat now. The walk from my room to rehab, which was just a few doors down, felt like miles. They had us get up on the treadmill and walk for just a couple of minutes at the pace of a snail, but it felt like torture. I kept my spirits by singing Amy Winehouse's "Rehab" as I made the trek. In addition to rehab, I was now on medications that they informed me that I may be on for the rest of my life. But I was alive! Now, I'm a lifetime pill popper.

I had a lot of time on my hands for the next week as I waited to be released from the hospital. I posted pictures and updates on Facebook. One of my friends appeared alarmed by my post announcing my stay in the hospital and upcoming surgery by asking me if I was serious. My reply: "I'm serious as a heart attack!" I do love a good play on words and irony. This picture freaked people out online. I had to unplug myself to go to the bathroom, and it looked like I was flat-lining. I posted, "Oh, no. I've flat-lined." Someone asked me, "Really?" How can I type this if I'm dead? Some people online aren't super smart.

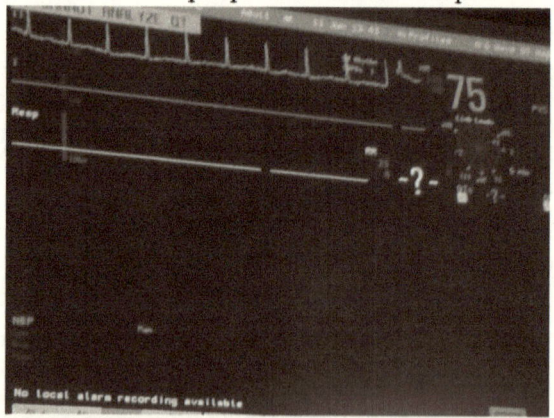

That much time on your hands in a confined space gives you a great opportunity to reflect and plan. I realized that life is not only too short, but it could end at any time. We are only here for a finite period of time. We need to make the most of it. Tomorrow is not guaranteed. Life is so precious and fragile. These phrases may sound very cliché, but nonetheless true. I was given a second chance, and I needed to do something with it.

We need to make the most of this time, because we do not know how much of it that we have. We do not need to spend a single second being unhappy. Now that being said, we cannot possibly be happy all of the time. We will experience sadness, anger, or stress from time to time. It is our reactions to these things that determine how long we will be unhappy. Life is too short to be in a relationship, job, friendship, or anything where we are not happy. We either need to change the situation or change how we react to the situation.

Before I could be discharged from the hospital, I had to have a bowel movement. Their rules, not mine. I sat in the bathroom for a while trying to make nature call. I had to drag my machine and all of its wires over to the door, but even on the other side of the door, I could hear the incessant beeps of the monitor. I brought in my phone and pulled up music to drown out that noise. I thought that Pantera could block the beeps, and I chose "Cemetery Gates", because I thought it would be creepy but still get the job done. Sure enough, mission accomplished. Music and humor got me through another tough situation.

According to a report from the U.S. Center for Disease Control and Prevention, heart disease is the leading cause of death in the U.S. and that number has stayed the same as the prior year. Heart disease is the number one killer in America, followed by cancer, according to the U.S. Centers for Disease Control and Prevention. In 2016, 633,842 people died from heart disease, followed by 595,930 from cancer.

There are a number of risk factors for heart disease. These risks can play a role in developing the disease, as well as, increasing your chances of making the existing disease worse. Among the various risk factors for heart disease include: genetics and stress.

One risk factor is if a person is genetically disposed to heart disease. There is not much that can be done about heredity, but knowledge of such a predisposition can allow you the opportunity to take preventative measures. However, there are risk factors that can be altered, such as high blood pressure, high cholesterol, an unhealthy diet, being overweight, and being inactive. Also, women after the age of 55 are more apt to get heart disease (and keep in mind that the heart attack symptoms in women can differ greatly from men). According to the Mayo Clinic, about half of all Americans have at least one of the three key risk factors for heart disease: high blood pressure, high cholesterol, and smoking.

Stress is also a significant risk factor, because unrelieved stress may damage your arteries and the heart itself. With today's busy lifestyle, coupled with inactivity, stress has become a common element of our daily lives. As we have learned, stress is the number one killer today.

There are several symptoms of heart issues, which may include: chest pain, sweating, a feeling of pressure or burning in the chest, irregular heartbeats, shortness of breath, and/or pain in the arm, back, or chest. But not all people experience the same signals. For instance, I felt the "elephant on the chest" and shortness of breath. I did not experience any pain, per se. Women typically have varying symptoms from men in regards to heart attacks. But any related symptoms should be taken very seriously, especially while participating in physical activity.

Measures that a heart patient may take to prevent and to improve their health would include proper exercise and diet, as well as getting regular check-ups with a medical professional and taking the proper medications. There are also other actions that the patient may take to aid in their health (of course, these alternative methods DO NOT take the place of medical assistance, but are advised to be used in conjunction as a complementary therapy).

Now having this surgery does not mean that I am out of the woods. I have to do check-ups each year and stress tests every few years. But research done at Aarhus University in Denmark shows that mortality increases after eight to ten years. According to the Mayo Clinic, most people may remain symptom-free for as long as up to ten to fifteen years, however, other arteries or even the new graft may become clogged. This would require another bypass or angioplasty. That is scary! I almost died, and I may die again. (Well, we all die, but ten years comes quickly!) Along with a healthy diet and regular exercise, the Mayo Clinic suggests that patients manage their stress. That hit home!

What do I know?

Some may ask what do I know about the subject of happiness? I do not have a doctorate in psychology. I didn't even study psychology other than a couple of classes in college. There are no cool titles or letters before or after my name. No Dr. Eidson or Christy Eidson, Ph.D. I'm just your average Joe. I finally found happiness, but it took a lot of work.

Now, I am not happy one hundred percent of the time. That is not realistic. But I have learned various ways of coping with the negatives when they pop up. I have spent half of my life suffering from depression and anxiety. I have lost jobs because of it, shut people out because of it, and even lost my home because of it. But I am not alone. According to the World Health Organization, one in four people worldwide will be affected by mental or neurological disorders at some point in their lives. Nearly one-quarter of the countries worldwide have no mental health legislation, and more than forty percent have no mental health policies at all.

In the United States, 16.2 million adults have at least one major depressive episode each year. Anxiety disorders affect 40 million adults in the United States each year. Anxiety even affects children, with twenty-five percent of children between 13 and 18 experiencing some sort of anxiety. There are many of us in the same boat. Anxiety and depression, along with stress, can, directly and indirectly, affect our general health and well-being.

In addition to dealing with depression and anxiety, I also have had to cope with a moderate amount of stress in my life. Add my issues with heart disease, and I am a champion of finding ways to reduce stress and increase happiness.

In the movie, Bob attempts to overcome his fears, indirectly, by seeking out his new psychiatrist who is on vacation. He meets Dr. Marvin's son, Siggy, who has fears of his own. One major fear that Siggy has is the fear of death.

Siggy: Bob, are you afraid of death?
Bob: (hesitates) Yeah.
Siggy: Me, too. There's no way out of it. You're going to die. I'm going to die. It's going to happen. What difference does it make if it's tomorrow or in eighty years? Much sooner in your case. Do you know how fast time goes? I was six like yesterday.
Bob: Me, too.
Siggy: I'm going to die. You…are going to die. What else is there to be afraid of?

Ironically, Dr. Marvin's "Death Therapy" cures Bob of his maladies. Death is one experience that we all must eventually face. There is no avoiding it. It is senseless to worry about things that you have absolutely no control over. That is stress with no resolution. Depression is worry about the past. Anxiety is worry about the future. If there is something in the future that you can do something about, then okay, worry. But if you cannot do anything about something, your worry is pointless. Worrying about things you cannot do anything about is totally futile and only leads to unnecessary stress.

"I'll sleep when I'm dead." ~ Warren Zevon

A Brief History of Stress and Drugs

Everyone experiences stress. It seems unavoidable. Stress is experienced by most people on a daily basis. Ever since the dawn of the Industrial Revolution, we have seen a huge rise in stress. But why? In a time when, due to strides in technology, we have more time available to us than ever before in history, yet we are more stressed. Even since the 1950s, there has been an even bigger surge in stress levels of individuals. Instead of technology giving us all this free time, we are exchanging that time for obtaining possessions and 'keeping up with the Joneses'.

In the pre-Industrial Era, people had very busy lifestyles farming, being in nature, raising families, and living in more rural areas. In the early 1800s, we saw a growth in the middle class. New forms of transportation, innovations in industry, and electricity all emerged changing the way that we lived our lives. The rail system changed how we traveled, and the telegraph in 1844 changed how we communicated and shared information. Thanks to industrialization, Americans had disposable income and more leisure time. Even with all of these changes, people were having difficulty adjusting to this new civilization. They were developing physical symptoms thought to be connected to the nervous system and believed to be a result of the higher demands of this new lifestyle.

The Civil War brought on new stresses. Over one million Americans were injured or killed during the war, which is roughly one-third of all those who served. War not only scars the body, but also scars the mind. Mental illness was viewed as a sign of weakness. Veterans exhibited war-related anxieties, and with the availability of opiates for pain and other ills, drug addiction became elevated. More people were killed by disease than bullets. After the war, many veterans exhibiting issues were committed to insane asylums or became the victim of suicide. Others turned to drinking heavily to mask their physical and mental pain.

Shortly after the Civil War, as the nation healed, industry boomed. The Transcontinental Railroad connected both coasts. Oil refining, steel manufacturing, developments in electricity and textiles, Ford's use of the assembly line, and the invention of the radio changed how Americans lived and worked. Towns and villages were turning into urbanized cities with workers moving into the areas for mining and manufacturing jobs. Areas were often segregated by class, with the working class living in the worst conditions. These areas were densely packed making disease easily spread. The industrial revolution saw a rise in accidents from industry and railways. Civil War soldiers developed traumatic stress reactions from battle. Due to the use of heavy explosives in World War I, soldiers developed symptoms of "shell shock". Soldiers were experiencing what we now call Post Traumatic Stress Disorder, or PTSD, and began noticing symptoms such as depression, anxiety, sleep problems, rapid pulse, and trouble breathing.

As the worst economic disaster in the history of the United States, the Great Depression lasted from 1929 to 1939. "Black Tuesday", as it is called, was October 29, 1929, and it marked the date that the stock market crashed. Within the first year of the Depression, thousands of banks closed. People in a panic withdrew their money from banks while others lost their money. Banks had also overextended credit to people. People lost their jobs due to layoffs, and repossessions and evictions were happening frequently. The unemployment rate rose to over twenty-five percent. People were making less and spending less. Tariffs were raised causing world trade to fall. On top of that, a drought-ravaged middle America, forcing people to move from the region due to economic collapse. The Dust Bowl caused massive dust storms, killed crops and livestock, and caused sickness in residents. Even though the Depression-era was a stressful time, people focused on their families and survival through one of the toughest periods in American history. Healthcare of the American people declined due to malnutrition, alcohol abuse, and even suicide. One industry that helped boost the American spirit was the movie industry. People were going to movies as an escape, but also for air conditioning!

World War II sent the men folk overseas, and women were pushed into industrial jobs to take up the slack left from the absent men. Women were taking factory and shipyard jobs in record numbers. They were even taking jobs that were traditionally held by men, such as engineers, chemists, and journalists. After the war, many women had sought to keep their jobs, but many were laid-off. One survey found that eighty percent of women responded that they wanted to retain their jobs after the war. Unfortunately, most did not. Overwhelming social pressure encouraged women to return to their roles of homemaker so that returning veterans could go back to their previous jobs. *"Here, ladies. We're going to give you a life and independence outside the home. You will have the feeling of equality with men by doing their jobs. Oh, wait. Just kidding. Get back into the kitchen!"*

With World War II, soldiers were labeled with having "battle fatigue", with soldiers becoming battle weary and exhausted. After World War II, we entered the 1950s, which was a time where we began to see what we now call the Nuclear Family. This was deemed the ideal, traditional family. Everyone strived for two-point-five kids and a house with a picket fence. The father worked at a job that he most likely would retire from at the age of 65. The mother stayed at home with the kids and tended the home duties.

This would appear to be a low-stress period, but with the introduction of the 1960s, diazepam was born. Diazepam, also known as Valium, became widely used and referred to as 'Mother's Little Helper'. Diazepam was used as a substitute for Barbiturates, which in the 1950s, was discovered to cause behavioral disturbances and physical dependency potential. Diazepam also had the potential for abuse and dependence, but was found less dangerous than other Barbiturates in that death rarely resulted from an overdose. *"Here, take this. At least you won't die...maybe."* Both depress the central nervous system, leading to a relaxed state. Diazepam has been commonly used to treat a variety of conditions ranging from anxiety and panic attacks to insomnia.

If you remember the 1966 song from the Rolling Stones, "Mother's Little Helper" refers to the drug Valium, which had become very popular at the time.

What a drag it is getting old
Kids are different today, I hear every mother say
Mother needs something today to calm her down
And though she's not really ill, there's a little yellow pill
She goes running for the shelter of a mother's little helper
And it helps her on her way, gets her through her busy day

*Written by Mick Jagger and Keith Richards, recorded at the RCA Record Studios in Hollywood, CA.

And even later on, the song warns of the danger of possible overdose.

Women during this time period were clearly more stressed than we thought. Women were being prescribed Valium twice as often as men. Why? Could it be because they felt unequal to their male partners? Could it be because they felt their lives were mundane and unfulfilled? The ambitions of the woman had to take a backseat to the tending to the family home.

Women are held at a different standard than men. Gender bias, the media's depiction of what the female form should be, and women being targeted in pharmaceutical marketing are just a few of the reasons for the history of women being excessively prescribed narcotics in comparison to men. In the late 1950s, women's magazines such as *Ladies' Home Journal* and *Cosmopolitan* were filled with articles about these miracle pills. They were touted to help women deal with everything from motherhood to working in a man's world. Your emotional ills could be cured by a quick visit to the doctor and getting a prescription for a pill.

Today, the Nuclear Family is not as present as it once was. Divorce is on the rise in America with almost fifty percent of all marriages ending in divorce or separation. And even if the Nuclear Family is intact, now both parents are working. Children are in daycare or afterschool care. Houses are larger. Two cars are now in the driveway. TVs have gotten bigger. Parents are eating out or picking up food from a drive-thru as they don't have time to cook dinner. Families aren't even talking at the dinner table anymore as technology has taken everyone's attention away from family time. Cellphones, television, and videogames have taken our attention away from each other.

Now more than ever, we need to find and implement methods to deal with stress in our lives.

Here are some ways:
- Laughter - The Mayo Clinic writes that laughter can "stimulate circulation and aid muscle relaxation, both of which help reduce some of the physical symptoms of stress."
- Get a pet or watch cute animal videos. No, seriously! - One paper from *Frontiers in Psychology* reviewed sixty-nine studies and concluded that interacting with animals lowers fear and anxiety in people. Part of the reason for this lies in oxytocin, a hormone that, among its other jobs, reduces stress. Interaction with animals pumps more oxytocin to your brain.
- Smile - Smiling helps lower stress, lowers heart rates, and actually makes you feel better.
- Exercise - Even if you are tired, exercising gives you more energy. It lowers stress and increases endorphins.
- Unplug from technology – it is proven that constant communication increases stress.
- Meditation - reduces stress, improves concentration, increases acceptance, and improves cardiovascular and immune health.
- Yoga - can lessen chronic pain, lower blood pressure, reduce insomnia, and increase flexibility.
- Tai chi - strengthens muscles, increases flexibility and balance, and lowers blood pressure.
- Forest bathing - It is scientifically proven that Shinrin-yoki, or forest bathing, boosts the immune system, increases NK cells, and reduces blood pressure.
- Reiki - reduces stress, brings about inner peace and harmony, balances mind and emotions, relieves pain, and speeds recovery from surgery and illness.
- Aromatherapy - Relieves stress, has an antidepressant capacity, increases memory, boosts energy levels, speeds

up healing and recovery, alleviates headaches and pain, enhances the immune system, and aids in sleep.

3 YOU ARE NOT YOUR CIRCUMSTANCES

"A pessimist sees the difficulty in every opportunity; an optimist sees the opportunity in every difficulty." ~ Winston Churchill

Growing Up

I grew up in a house without central heat and air or indoor plumbing. I was raised by my great grandparents. We lived on social security. We were beyond poor. My mother died when I was five, and I didn't know my father. I have worked a ton of dead-end jobs and unfulfilling occupations. I suffer from anxiety and depression. I have had chronic insomnia. I would drink alcohol to self-medicate. I had a heart attack. I was faced with a lot of unhappiness.

I am not a doctor. I am not a psychologist or a social worker. I am not a motivational guru…yet. I put myself through college with grants, scholarships, and unfortunately, student loans. I am a comedian, actor, writer, and producer. I am a single mother and pet owner. I am a business owner with my own successful sightseeing tour company. I have just written my first book! I have started to build my Youtube channel. I am learning a new language and an instrument. I am learning to cope with my stresses and develop techniques to make myself happy and find joy.

Now, you know a little bit about me. I did not allow myself to be a victim of my circumstances. I realized that happiness is not outside of ourselves. Happiness resides within us all. It comes from the inside. We already have what we need to make ourselves happy. It is a matter of perspective.

I grew up in a small town in Tennessee called Millersville. It was so small that it didn't even have a traffic light. But why would it? There was only one main road: Old Louisville Highway, or 31W as city folks called it. We lived in a little white house right off that road. We did not have running water, so as you can imagine, we had no bathroom. We had an outhouse, and we had what you would call a bedpan. I called it a bucket. Nothing was worse than having to go to the bathroom in it, and if you couldn't go right away and had to sit there for any length of time, you had a thin but deep and painful crease at the top of your thighs, right below your butt-cheeks. Not a pretty picture I know, but one I felt I had to paint nonetheless. But I chose that bucket over getting up in the middle of the night and putting on a jacket and shoes to go to the outhouse any day! In the winters, the outhouse was cold! And in the summers, there would always manage to be some sort of bees nest in or around the outhouse (wood bees, wasps, hornets), and I am not a fan of things that sting…especially with my butt exposed.

The den was where we spent most of our time, because it is where the wood stove was. The stove was our source of heating in the winter. Since this was our source of heating, the den is where we slept as well. I would sometimes help my great grandfather tote the wood from the woodpile to the front porch, where we kept it for the next day's use. I loved helping my great grandfather and would follow him everywhere he went. He would take me to the store with him. Every time we went, he would stop and talk to someone. We would go to get a loaf of bread, and we would be in the store for three hours. When I was little, I thought he must know everyone in the world, because he never seemed to meet anyone that he didn't know. He would usually buy me candy while we were there, so that was more incentive for me to go with him.

The den was also where I spent most of my time because that is the room that had the television in it. My great grandparents were older, as you can imagine. They were tired from raising five children of their own, plus my mother, and now me, so I spent a great deal of my childhood in front of the television. It was pretty much my babysitter. It stayed on from the moment we woke up until we went to bed. Yes, Jamie Summers, the Addams family, Gilligan, Diana/Wonder Woman, the Munsters, J.J., Fred Sanford, and Archie Bunker all had a hand in raising me. This, also, explains a lot.

Being poor

My mother died when I was five, and her mother died when she was young, so I was raised by my great grandparents. Once they reached retirement age, they relied on their social security checks. There were no 401(k), no savings, no stocks, no bonds, no t-bills. I don't even know what a t-bill is. Stocks? Why would you put money in something that you could lose? That's the same as gambling, and to them, that was a sin. But not only that, they didn't have money left over to risk. Can you imagine living on under $800 a month? We did it for a family of three. From time to time, my family would have to use government assistance.

We may have been poor, but we were proud. My great grandparents did not believe in or acquire debt if they could help it.

They never had a credit card, a new car, or loans of any kind. The only debt they ever acquired was hospital bills. But it is not like they were eager to go to the doctor. I can only remember going to the doctor once as a child, and that was to get my immunizations to start school. My great grandmother never went. My great grandfather started going to the doctor after his first heart attack. Notice I said first. He had a few over the course of his retirement age. The second heart attack resulted in heart surgery with six by-passes.

I loved summertime. For the beginning of summer, we would get out the scissors and cut off all my old school pants to make shorts. If my shoes had gotten too small, we would even cut the toes off of them. They would be kind of makeshift sandals, I suppose. I spent most of my summers on the porch or in the yard. As soon as the dew would dry on the grass, my great grandmother would send me out, with my instructions to keep on my shoes, not to climb any trees, and not to get near the road. In her mind, a car might lose control and wildly go off the road and into our front yard, ramming into the tree, and knocking me out of the tree as a swarm of bees savagely attacked my bare feet.

When I was in the fifth-grade, there was a charity that gave shopping sprees of fifty dollars to underprivileged children. I was a recipient. But instead of being excited about it, I was upset by it. Did that mean that I was underprivileged? And if so, now others would know that I am underprivileged. I hated for other people to know I was poor, and I hated to think of myself as poor. I just thought we were living under differing conditions is all. Not that we were lesser than everyone else. After the shopping spree to Hills Department Store, which is no longer around, the buses all took us back to the school. We were running around and playing while we waited for our parents to pick us up. I was running and turned to look behind me. As I turned around, wham! I ran into the back of another kid's head. I gave him a whopper with my teeth, and consequently, I bit my own tongue in half. Literally, it was bitten in half, with just a small piece of flesh holding it on. Needless to say, I was freaking out! Blood was everywhere. We both were crying.

When my great grandparents got to the school, the chaperone told them what had happened. Do you think they rushed me to the hospital? No. "Hey, where are you going? The hospital is that way", I thought to myself. We went right back to the house, and my great grandmother stuck a towel in my mouth to stop the bleeding. All the while, I'm wondering how I'm going to survive without a tongue. No more licking ice cream. No more sticking my tongue out at people. No licking stamps. And forget sticking my tongue out and touching my nose. Wait…am I going to be able to talk again??? Noooooo! As crazy as I thought my great grandmother was, she must have known my tongue would grow back together on its own. And it did. She only had a fifth grade education herself. I was in fifth grade, and I didn't know that about the tongue at the time. I ate only soup and ice cream for a week, but at the end of the week, my tongue was completely intact, if not a little longer as a result. I now have a tongue that could give Gene Simmons a run for his money. I didn't know if my great grandparents relied so heavily on home remedies because they knew they would work or because they didn't have the money to go to the hospital. Luckily for me, the home remedies worked.

Hand-me-downs
Most of the clothes that I ever had growing up were hand-me-downs. Do you remember your first grade picture? I do. I was wearing this maroon, polyester pantsuit with polka dots. Sweet! Highly flammable polyester…one spark from my grandma's cigarette, and I might not be here today. My hair was in pigtails – with the hair ties with two huge plastic balls on each end. I don't

think you can even buy these anymore, for legal reasons. My forehead all stretched out. It looked like I had a bad facelift. Kids would yank on them and make motorcycle sounds. Of course, I'd get back at them by using my ponytails like nunchucks and whipping my head around and slapping them in the eye with my ponytail. Good times. By the time I was in third grade, I was deadly accurate.

They say that your best times in life are when you're a child. I say that's a damn lie. Because let's fast forward to fifth grade. I have been getting hand-me-downs, from my cousin – my boy cousin. The feathered shag haircut was in at the time, like Rick Springfield. My older female cousin got it – short in the front, party in the back - the birth of the mullet. My grandma decides to get my hair cut in a shag…a short shag. Now I love Rick Springfield, but I didn't want to look like Rick Springfield. So I go from my long, motorcycle handlebar ponytails to looking like a boy. In fifth grade, I had no boobs yet and was wearing boy clothes with a boy haircut.

I was an only child growing up and had to play by myself a lot. My grandma didn't want other kids to come over much. "If someone got hurt, they could sue us." Sue us, and take all this – a four-room house built in the pre-civil war era, with a wood stove for heat, and a rusty, short-circuiting fan for cooling that would spontaneously burst into flames for no reason, and no running water. Yes, no running water. I felt like Tiny Tim growing up. You'd think the 80's I grew up in were the 1880's. When I hear people talking about growing up poor, I think, you don't know poor until you've had to put on shoes and a coat to go to the bathroom. Either that or poop in a bucket. That's poor. One thing though, we never had to worry about mice or bugs or anything like that…because they couldn't live in those conditions.

School

The best part about elementary school was also the worst part of elementary school: substitutes. Substitutes usually mean a free day, which is great! But at the beginning of the day, as they call the roll, they also collect your lunch money. I received free lunch at school, so all of us free lunch kids, which there were usually only five or six of us, had to call out "free lunch" instead of walking up to the teacher's desk with our money. That was just humiliating. In middle school, it was a lot better. At the beginning of the week, we would go to the cafeteria before school began, and we would get our "free lunch" cards. Awesome! Now, no one would really know that we had free lunch. It was a facet of our lives we could hide more easily. In high school, I refused to be humiliated any more. I qualified for free lunch still, but chose to pay for my lunch instead. A high school girl needs her dignity!

Nature, Nurture, or Choice?

Why am I telling you all of this? Why am I sharing so much about my dark underbelly? It is because I believe that there are a lot of people out there that can relate to my story. The details may differ, but we all have had our struggles. Some of us have had less privileged lives than others. I am here as proof that you can change your life and overcome your circumstances. You are not defined by your situation.

According to my circumstances, you would think that I would be trapped in an endless cycle of poverty and lack of education. But I made the decision to change my situation. I always was at the top of my class even in elementary school. I made the conscious choice to go to college. I did not have the money, let alone know how to apply for college, but I was determined. Thanks to scholarships and grants, I was able to go.

Now, I will be the first to say that it was not easy. After my sophomore year of college, my great grandfather died. My family sold the home that I had lived in, so now I had to find a new place to live. During my junior year, I became pregnant. Suddenly, I became responsible for another human being. I had to take out loans to keep myself in school, food on the table, and a roof over our heads. It took me much longer to finish college, but I did it. College and my child were important to me. So to get the life that I wanted, I had to make them my top priorities.

I may not be a psychologist or a licensed therapist. I may not be a self-help guru being interviewed by Oprah (at least not yet), but I have learned a few things about life. In the end, only you are responsible for you. You can blame your parents, your schools, your upbringing, your situation, your disadvantages, but in the end, it all falls on you and only you.

For a long time, there has been the debate over which influences someone's personality more: nature or nurture. Nature refers to your genes. Nurture refers to your childhood or how you were brought up. Basically, nature is biological, whereas nurture is social and environmental.

If my path followed Nature, which refers to my genetic make-up including my physical appearance and personality characteristics, or if my path followed Nurture, which refers to all of the environmental variables such as my childhood experiences, relationships, culture, and rearing, the outcome would most likely have been the same. If I had followed the path of most of the people in my family as well as my community, I would have never gone to college. I would have been married immediately after high school and started popping our children. I would have been a stay-at-home mom, possibly getting a "little job" as soon as the kids were big enough. Once they were grown, the cycle would start all over again with me babysitting my new grandkids. Now, for those who choose to do this, there is nothing wrong with this. However, that lifestyle did not appeal to me or my dreams.

It is for these reasons that I suggest that there is another option: Freewill. I believe that my scenario shows that we have a choice as to how we end up. It is a matter of how we play the cards that we are dealt.

The meaning of life

When one door closes, another one opens. When one life ends, another begins. For everything taken away, something new is given. For every ending, there is a beginning. From every death, there is a rebirth. All the clichés make sense. Life is constantly changing. And with it, so shall we change and transform. Our bodies, our lives, our families, our thoughts, our beliefs, our worlds all modify and metamorphose over time. You can choose to dwell on the negatives and the losses. Or you can choose to see the glass as half full and enjoy the gifts that are there to find. When my great grandfather died, I could have wallowed in the loss of him, my home, my possessions, and I did for a while, but then I would have missed the big picture. My priorities had changed. Possessions and petty bickering did not matter anymore. I did not care what anyone thought, except for my daughter. She was all that mattered.

All that matters is having someone or something to care for, support, and love. We are put here to help those in need and to love one another. Is that the meaning of life? How simple and obvious is that? That is what is really important. The amount of love and care in your heart is the measure of a good life and a life well-lived. Loneliness is the antithesis of this. Could this be why dating sites, social media, and most things on the internet are so successful, because it feeds that need that we all have for a personal connection with other people? No one wants to be lonely.

THE HEART OF HAPPINESS

We all want some sort of connection, even if it is a virtual one.

"And, in the end the love you take is equal to the love you make."
~ Paul McCartney of the Beatles

4 CHANGE YOUR BRAIN

"As you think, so shall you become." ~ Bruce Lee

What is Neuroplasticity?
The brain has an amazing ability to grow and to expand. It was commonly thought that the brain is fully developed after the first few years of life, but scientists are discovering that is not true at all. It was believed that the connections formed between the brain's nerve cells were fixed as we age. Neuroplasticity proves this incorrect. According to MedicineNet.com, "Neuroplasticity allows the neurons (nerve cells) in the brain to adapt and compensate for injury and disease and to adjust their activities in response to new situations or to changes in their environment." We now know that the brain is continually adjusting and reorganizing itself and forming new neural connections, and this continues throughout our lives.

Neuroplasticity is the brain's ability to form new neural connections throughout life. It allows the neurons in the brain to compensate for injury or disease. Even if one's brain becomes damaged, it can create new pathways to be able to function properly. It is our brain's ability to repair connections or find alternative pathways. This could include pathways to memories, emotions, and physical systems. For instance, if a person had a traumatic injury which resulted in a loss of speech, neuroplasticity would allow their brains to develop new neural pathways to regain verbal communication again. When we repeat a thought or emotion, we reinforce a neural pathway. If repeated frequently enough, these changes create changes in how our brains work. Like with any muscle, the more that we work it, the stronger it gets. This is true for the brain with neuroplasticity. An example would be when we begin to learn to play a musical instrument. With enough repetition, the chords become automatic. Playing the instrument becomes second nature.

Brain cell survival, including the formation of connections, can be determined by genetics, environmental conditions, social interactions, experiences, and even fresh air. Just like nerve cells can change in response to environmental conditions, they can change in response to injury or disease as well. Likewise, if one hemisphere of the brain is damaged, the other hemisphere will sometimes take over some of the functions of the damaged side. Even though these connections are being made, they still have to be stimulated. Without stimulations, these areas of the brain will not improve and the impairment will continue. With that, it is important to stimulate the neurons in order for them to remain active. This will allow them to continue to form new connections and promote rehabilitation. According to the Neuroplasticity article written by Stephanie Liou from Stanford University, "A first key principle of neuroplasticity is this: brain activity promotes brain reorganization. In other words, 'brain workouts' help the brain reorganize connections more quickly and stimulate reorganization when the brain is not capable of reorganizing on its own."

In addition, it is believed that an active lifestyle helps to maintain brain function. This is why older people are encouraged to do crossword and word search puzzles, as they are exercises for the brain. Constant stimulation of the brain is believed to ward off dementia and other mentally debilitating illnesses. Being active in general is exceptionally beneficial for older people to maintain longevity.

Mind Over Matter

Life is mind over matter: "if you don't mind, it don't matter". I think that we have all heard that saying. It is a principle that deals with the basis of perception. Our reality is dependent on how we perceive things. If we believe it, it becomes true to us. That is why positive or negative thinking has such a powerful influence on our minds. One can have a pessimistic outlook, and the result may be stress and worry. Conversely, if one adopts a more optimistic outlook, the result is most likely positive. And even if it is not positive, we do not allow it to bother us. Any conflicts that arise, we have the confidence to deal with it head-on. If it is a conflict that we have no control over, then we let the problem roll off of us like the water off of a duck's back. We do not allow it to consume us, and therefore, stress us.

It could have been easy for me to have been stuck in the mindset that I was poor and would always be poor, but I reprogrammed my thinking. It was not easy, and it took a lot of time, but I eventually came to the realization that if I had a good, well-thought-out plan, I could give myself the gift of a better life.

One way to reprogram the brain is to refrain from negative labeling. If you think you are poor, you will be. If you believe that you can't do something, you won't be able to. To reverse this, give yourself a positive label: "I am a successful business owner" or "I am a talented, gifted writer."

When one's life is riddled with tragedy and strife, it is easy to wallow in a giant pity party. The mind can become flooded with the images of all of the things that we don't have in our lives. It is easy to own the label of "victim", but that label limits us and shines a negative light on our disadvantages. But if we refuse to look at them as disadvantages, but rather as opportunities, we change our label from "victim" to "survivor", or even "warrior"!

Two people are taking a cooking class, but they are both struggling. They both were having a difficult time making a soufflé. Both soufflés ended up burned and deflated. The first student beats himself up about it by saying, "I'm a failure. I can't do anything right. There is nothing that I'm good at." The second student thinks, "I've never been much of a cook, but this class is fun. Considering that I have never spent much time in a kitchen, I didn't do too terrible of a job, and I've learned a lot from my mistakes with this recipe." One exhibits a negative thought process, and the other displays a more positive one. Both of them had the same experiences and results, but their perspectives on them were different.

The brain is the most complex organ in the body. It is baffling how much power the mind has over the body. The body's ability to heal itself is quite remarkable. Proof in this is when people miraculously get better after taking placebo drugs instead of taking actual pharmaceuticals. They do not realize that they are taking a sugar pill, but rather their minds think they are taking actual medicine that will make them better. When a patient takes a medication with the expectation that it will benefit them, it typically does, but is it due to the medicine or does positive thinking play a role?

These are not just theories as there has been much research on the topic. PET scanners and MRIs have been used to look at the brain activity of patients, and these tests have shown the brain's positive response to the placebo. Researchers discovered that the thought processes of these patients lead to changes in their brain chemistry, which led to visible physical changes in the patient.

Shit Happens

To live a life with reduced stress, you must adopt a passive attitude. This is especially true for the things in life that you cannot control. In the philosophy of Taoism, you must be like water in the stream. The water flows freely and does not fight against or try to go through the stone in the stream. It bends itself to flow around the rock.

Because it is inevitable that we will face some bumps in the road from time to time, to keep our sanity, you must adopt a passive attitude. There is no sense in worrying about things that you cannot do anything about. You must learn to let go of the things that you cannot control.

In the movie *The Big Lebowski*, the Dude has bad break after bad break, but he never loses his cool. He gets his rug urinated on, insulted, his car stolen, his rug stolen, and his friend dies, but he remains calm, cool, and collected. He learned that "sometimes you eat the bar, and sometimes the bar eats you." He found ways of dealing with stress like taking a bubble bath and drinking white Russians. He had a support system with Donnie and Walter. He stayed active with hobby by bowling on a league against Jesus. He may not have had money for rent, but he did not allow himself to worry over things that he had no control over. And in the end, everything worked out for the Dude. He went with the flow and found happiness within himself.

Be Positive

In the world that we live in, it is sometimes difficult to be positive.

The news can be flooded with negativity. Even reading your social media feed can be a downer. But we have to remember that pessimism is not good for your health. Negative thinkers have higher rates of depression. Pessimists have higher levels of heart disease and do not live as long as more optimistic people. Optimists also experience greater productivity at work than their counterparts.

There are only two ways to look at things: Positively or Negatively. But we have to realize that the phrase "stay positive" is much more than just wishful thinking. It is a matter of rewiring our brains. We have been conditioned to accept and expect negativity, and it does not have to be that way. When we experience failures, instead of taking it personally, we need to look at them as learning experiences. Nothing is a mistake if we can learn something from it.

One way to become more positive is to learn to take a compliment. Some people cannot accept praise or compliments. Sometimes our negative self-talk will not allow ourselves to take positive reinforcement seriously. When I was fourteen, I went through that typical awkward teenage phase. I overheard my great grandmother tell my cousin that I was unattractive. I was vulnerable, and that was devastating. Granted, she was a senile old woman, but this was someone that I trusted. I took that opinion as fact, so when anyone else said anything nice about my appearance, I quickly dismissed it. This is a harsh example, but it goes to show that opinion is not fact. It also proves that everything is impermanent. Phases come and go, and I ultimately grew out of that period, but the negative self-talk stayed. If I had not changed my thinking and hushed my negative self-talk, I would never have been able to take a compliment from someone.

Set boundaries. With that experience with a family member, I learned at an early age that I had to set boundaries for myself and for others. I could not allow someone else's negativity to influence my opinion of myself. You can love someone and still establish boundaries with them. The most important person in your life is you, and your opinion of yourself is the only one that matters.

The difference between being positive or negative can depend on as little as the wording. One has to turn **"Yeah, but"** into **"Yes, and**…" If someone asks you if you like to go bowling, instead of saying "yeah, but I'm not very good at it", say "Yes, and I have joined a bowling league so that I can get better and make new friends." *"Yes, but"* gives excuses for not pursuing a goal or completing a task. It reflects a lack of confidence and appears weak. *"Yes, and..."* on the other hand, comes across as assertive and strong.

Words have strength, and they can change the meaning of what is trying to be conveyed. The negative self-talk can be subtle. "CAN'T" never could; "WILL" always had to do it. The more that you believe that you can do something, the more likely you will do it. The more you do something successfully, the more you believe that you will be able to do it again. The opposite is also true: the more you believe that you cannot do something, the less likely you will do it. If you don't think you can do something, you're right. Your negative self-talk becomes a self-fulfilling prophecy.
Take these phrases, for instance:
> "I can't" – You're right!
> "I might" – No, you won't.
> "I should" – Then you really don't want to.
> "I'll try" – There is no try. There is do or do not.
> "I will" – Good. You're getting there.
> "I am" – Yes!

When verbalizing your goals, to create a positive visualization, don't say "I want to be a writer." Say with confidence, "I AM a writer." Give yourself the distinction and own it! "I will write a book" is not as definitive as "I AM writing a book."

Celebrate your successes. Even if they may seem small to others, any action gets you closer to success. Every success gets you closer to reaching your goal. Celebrating successes makes you feel good about yourself, and when you feel good about yourself, you become happy.

Take an inventory of your strengths. What do you like about yourself? What would other people say that they like about you? This is not a conceited exercise. You are not arrogant by bragging on yourself. This is an exercise to help build your confidence in your skills and talents. Make a list of all of your strengths and be proud of them. No one else is like you.

You are the company that you keep. If you surround yourself with negative people, it is no surprise that you may become negative. Negativity leads to anxiety and depression. Who you surround yourself with determines your quality of life. Most successful people are positive, optimistic people. Align yourself with the people that you want to be like.

Do more of what you like to do. Get involved in volunteering. Take up a hobby. Join a team. Take a class that interests you. You should always be learning. You should always stay active. Get moving. Get off the couch and exercise more. Walking is easy and takes no special equipment and not a lot of time.

Refrain from drugs and alcohol. These things may mask your pain for a moment, but when their effects subside, you may feel even worse than you did before. Drugs and alcohol abuse can have an adverse effect on your health as well as your judgment. And in the end, they may make your problem seem worse than it was before.

Eating healthy does the opposite. When your body is properly nourished, you feel better. Feeling good leads to happiness. Making sure that you are getting enough sleep also puts you in that good feeling state.

Like smiling or yawning, positivity is contagious, and it grows. The more positive one is the more positive those around him become. It is like ripples in a pond. When you drop the smallest pebble in a pond of still water, the ripples start small, but as they spread out, they become bigger and bigger.

Some people are wired to be more optimistic than others, but optimism can be learned. Being positive is just mind over matter. If you don't mind, it doesn't matter. It does not mean that you don't care about things, but rather that you find ways of coping with hardships. Your past has made you the person that you are. Even the bad stuff has made you a stronger person.

What can you do to be more positive and happy in general?
- Stop watching the news! I know you think that we should know what is going on in the world, but watching the news every day is a catalyst for anxiety, stress, and depression.
- Get off Social Media! Yes, we all need to stay connected, but how many hours do you waste each week (even day) mindlessly scrolling through your feed. How many times did you pick up your phone to check posts? How many times do you get angry or upset about what you see?
- Get connected in real life. Get off your devices and talk to the person in front of you. Actively listen.

"Love yourself first and everything else falls into line." ~ Lucille Ball

Positive Affirmations

"Each morning when I open my eyes I say to myself: I, not events, have the power to make me happy or unhappy today. I can choose which it shall be." ~ Groucho Marx

Now that you have turned your negative self-talk into positive, we are going to take it to the next level. If we use positive thoughts about ourselves, we can create a very powerful effect. Affirmations are positive statements that can help you to overcome your self-sabotaging thought patterns. If repeated often, one can evoke a positive change in their lives. If something is repeated often enough, it becomes a habit. If you do repetitive physical exercises, you will soon notice a difference in your muscle tone. The same can be done with your brain and thought composition. We can reprogram our thought patterns, and soon, we will be feeling and behaving differently.

Positive affirmations are the pep talks that we give ourselves. If you remember the character Stuart Smalley from Saturday Night Live, Al Franken's character used daily affirmations to boost his self-esteem. His most popular affirmation was: "I'm good enough, I'm smart enough, and doggone it, people like me!"

Affirmations can boost your confidence, improve your self-esteem, and increase your productivity. They can put your negative emotions in check. They are quite effective on their own, but even more so when paired with other techniques. They go hand-in-hand with visualization exercises to add a verbal element to the visual component. Affirmations are great to use along with goal setting techniques. It is important to be repetitive with affirmations. Repeat them several times each day.

Think about what you would like to change. Make sure that the affirmation that you choose is realistic. Saying "I'm going to double my income next week" may not be achievable. Make sure that they are positive and in the present tense. Not "I'm going to", but rather "I am". Make sure there is emotion invested in your affirmation to give it strength. You need to believe it. "I AM capable."

Here are some examples of positive affirmations:
1) I can do this.
2) I am creative.
3) I am successful.
4) My peers respect me and value my opinion.
5) I am grateful for my home and job.
6) I am happy and excited.
7) I exude positivity and enthusiasm.
8) I am a kind person and I deserve love.
9) I am a beautiful person.
10) I love myself unconditionally.
11) I am fearless, strong, and passionate.
12) I am calm and peaceful.
13) I am aware of my full potential.
14) There is no obstacle that I cannot overcome.
15) Life is beautiful and amazing.
16) I only attract positivity into my life.
17) I am a better me today than I was yesterday.
18) I am content. I am good enough.
19) There is no limitation on what I can achieve.
20) I am creating the path to my dreams.

Each night when I go to bed, I always tell myself how grateful I am for my bed. I slept on the same mattress for the first twenty years of my life, and who knows who slept on it and for how long before me. After that, I always bought cheap mattresses, and they did the job. But a few years ago, I decided that I was worth it and made the splurge to buy a good, quality mattress. It has helped with my chronic insomnia, so I reinforce my gratitude by expressing my thanks each night before I go to sleep.

Write your positive affirmations down and put them in a place where you will see them often. Put the affirmations on post-it notes on your bathroom mirror or refrigerator. Use a cork board or dry erase board to display your affirmations. Repetition is the key. See how I am repeatedly repeating the need for repetition?

Fostering Motivation
"Be miserable. Or motivate yourself. Whatever has to be done, it's always your choice". ~ Wayne Dyer

Happiness has a direct correlation to motivation which leads to productivity. The Harvard Business Review conducted a study that found that people are more productive when they are positive. Thus, one can assume that having a positive outlook and being happy makes people more motivated.

When one loses motivation, it is typically due to one of three reasons: 1) a lack of confidence, 2) a lack of focus, or 3) a lack of direction. When one has a lack of confidence, they do not believe that they can succeed, so they don't even try. When there is a lack of focus, one does not know what they want to do. It is difficult for them to realize what they really want to do. Lastly, if there is a lack of direction, they don't know how to do it. If one doesn't know what to do, they will not be motivated to do it.

To get more motivated, one must boost their confidence. Eliminating negative self-talk is one way to start. One may begin to focus on what they do not have or what they are lacking. One may become jealous or make excuses as to why they cannot succeed. When this occurs, one must begin to focus on gratitude. Be grateful for what you do have and what your strengths are.

Think of your past successes and current advantages. Increasing your confidence will get you motivated to build on your current success.

A lack of focus is a detriment to motivation. We may often focus on what we do not want instead of what we do want. One must focus on a positive goal instead of a vague fear. The law of attraction comes into play here. Instead, focus on what you do want to come into your life. Clearly defining your goal will determine your actions steps. Once you have concrete and measurable steps, you can move forward. Devising a plan is the first step toward taking action.

Now that you have confidence and focus, you must gain direction. Direction is your strategy of achieving your goal. If you do not know what your next action should be, you may be more inclined to procrastinate. A good example is if one wants to be a writer, but they spend more time researching topics or other writers instead of sitting down and typing or putting pen to paper. If you want to be a good guitar player, of course, it is good to take note of the great guitar players. But to be a good guitar player yourself, you must actually play!

There is an order to your goal.
1. First, you learn the parts of the guitar.
2. Next, you learn how to properly tune your guitar.
3. Then, you would learn your scales and chords.
4. Before long, you will be learning to play actual songs.
5. The more that you practice, the better you will be.

What if you just don't feel motivated? Just do it! Fake it until you make it. Get started and the motivation will follow. People mistakenly think that motivation leads to action, but the opposite is true. Once we take action, we become motivated. Start with a small task, and once it is complete, it will create momentum to pursue another task. If your motivation wanes, maybe you need to rethink or reorganize your plan. Motivation takes discipline. To achieve a goal, it is vital that you maintain discipline as well as motivation. Start with a small step if the big goal seems overwhelming. If you want to do a marathon, start by just running for three minutes. Start small and build up! This will build momentum, and consistency will create a habit. Small actions will snowball into bigger accomplishments.

Make a list of what needs to be done, and then set yourself up so that you cannot fail. For example, if you want to go to the gym every morning, go to bed in your gym clothes. Have your gym shoes by the bed. When you get up in the morning, you are ready to go. If you want to eat healthier, get rid of the junk food in your home. If you get hungry, your only options will be healthy ones without all of the temptations.

Put your money where your mouth is! To ensure your commitment, make yourself a wager. Give yourself a concrete goal with a timeline, and monitor your progress until it is done. Put some money on the line. If you fail, you must donate fifty dollars to charity. If you succeed, keep the fifty dollars, and you can give yourself a treat like a pedicure. Of course, make sure any treats that you give yourself are positive ones. (If you are trying to lose weight, don't treat yourself for losing ten pounds by ordering a piece of cake.) This will give you consequences for your actions or lack thereof. A method such as this will help your progress in creating a habit.

Do you love what you want to do? Money is not a strong motivator. If you are passionate about what you want, you are more motivated to take action. What you are doing should be fulfilling and satisfying. If you are doing something that you love, it is easier to get out of bed in the morning. Instead of thinking of a task as something that you have to do, think of it as something that you get to do!

Get in the mood! If you want to inspire motivation, put on some music that gets you moving. A little "Thunderstruck" by AC/DC will get your heart racing. "We Will Rock You" by Queen will get you on your feet. Put on your jam and get to doin'! Unlike TV or the computer, music can be less distracting but give you the white noise you need to keep the clutter of your mind down.

If you are still having trouble getting motivated, go back to the beginning. Ask yourself why this is your goal. If you cannot answer why you are doing something, then you should reevaluate if this is truly something that you want to do. When developing goals, you must come up with the: who, what, when, where, why, and how. Of these, the WHY is the most important to figure out.

Gratitude

Gratitude is an emotion expressing appreciation for what one has. It is more than just saying "thank you", because its meaning goes deeper. When one practices gratitude, they reflect on what they are thankful for. Some may refer to this as "counting your blessings". It is acknowledging that life is good. True gratitude is a selfless act that is done unconditionally, but it can be contagious. It can also be quite cathartic.

The benefits of expressing gratitude are numerous. People practicing gratitude may experience positive emotions, sleep better, and have less depression and anxiety. Their immune systems may become stronger, and they may express more kindness and compassion.

Take a moment each day to notice new things that you are grateful for. Start a gratitude journal. It may change the way that you perceive situations. When you are relaxed and feeling good, you are happier. When you have your negative emotions in check, you are happier. Gratitude for healthy relationships and more social interactions leads to a happier life. People can sense when you are thankful and gracious. People are attracted to that. Gratitude makes you less materialistic, because you are content with what you already have. You become more optimistic, and your self-esteem increases. You realize that it's not all about you. When you sleep better, exercise more, and eat healthy, you are not only happier, but you also live longer. When you are grateful, your productivity increases, your decision making is improved, and you achieve your goals!

Gratitude leads to happiness.

How do you practice gratitude?
- Take five minutes each day to write in a gratitude journal. Just five minutes will make a difference.
- Make a gratitude jar…or box or can. Each day, write down on a little slip of paper three things that you are grateful for. Do this every day until your jar is full.
- Go for a walk. Walking is a great stress reliever. It can be quite cathartic as well. As you walk, take time to look at the trees, flowers, houses, and people around you. Find things along your walk that you are thankful for. And while you are on this walk, smile at the people that you pass by. Really observe your surroundings. Notice the textures, colors, sounds, and smells of your environment. Be aware of nature. Stop and smell the roses!
- Practice mindfulness meditation. Sit in a quiet place and reflect on what you are grateful for.
- Send a message of gratitude. Whether it is a phone call, email, text, or a handwritten letter, let someone know that

you are grateful for them. It will help you appreciate them, and it will mean a great deal to the recipient. This will help strengthen your social bond with them, as well. Express how your life has been benefitted from having this person in it.
- Make a collage. Much like a vision board, make a collage of the things that you are grateful for. Visualizing your gratitude will have a greater impact than just writing the words down on paper.
- Say "thank you" and really mean it! Not only is it good manners, but it will also make the recipient happy. It shows thoughtfulness and consideration.
- Prayer. If you are religious in nature, say a prayer of gratitude.

Random Acts of Kindness

Much like Mindfulness and Gratitude, doing Random Acts of Kindness allows one to be in the moment and appreciative. Most of us can get caught up in our busy lives that we forget to pay attention to the little things. One small, seemingly insignificant act may not appear considerable at the moment, but may mean a great deal to someone who is having a bad day or feels down on their luck. Little things can mean a lot. The world would be a much different place if everyone took the time and effort to do something, no matter how small, for someone else every day.

Do a good deed for the day. Go out of your way to make someone else's day a little bit better. Open the door for someone. Give someone a smile, hug, or compliment. Do at least one each day for a week. Make someone else's day better.

Here is a list of some examples:
1. Give someone a compliment, even a stranger.
2. Volunteer at a homeless shelter.

3. Volunteer at an animal shelter.
4. Donate extra dog or cat food to an animal shelter.
5. Do a marathon for a good cause.
6. Pick up litter.
7. Let someone go in front of you in line.
8. Donate blood.
9. Pay for someone's meal at a restaurant.
10. Donate your old clothes to charity.
11. Hold the elevator for someone.
12. Do yard work for your neighbor.
13. Pay for someone else's latte at a coffee shop.
14. Spread some positivity online.
15. Snap a photo for a couple trying to take a selfie.
16. Perform at a retirement home.
17. Leave a generous tip for a server.
18. Mentor a child.
19. Tutor a student.
20. Recycle.
21. Post inspirational notes around the office.
22. Leave quarters at the laundromat or carwash.
23. Hold the door open for someone.
24. Make someone laugh.
25. Really listen to someone.
26. Let one car merge in front of you in traffic.
27. Have a conversation with a stranger.
28. Read to a child.
29. Visit someone who may be lonely.
30. Did you get good service today? Let the manager know.
31. Smile and say hello to a stranger.
32. Send an email to someone showing them your gratitude.
33. Give recognition to a co-worker. Let them know that they are doing a good job.
34. Return shopping carts at the grocery store to make less work for the employees.
35. While you're out, compliment a parent on how well-behaved their child is.

36. Pay the toll for the person behind you.
37. Learn the names of the people you see every day (bank teller, security guard,etc.).
38. Keep an extra umbrella at work, so you can lend it out when it rains.
39. Put your phone away while in the company of others.
40. Email or write to a former teacher who made a difference in your life.

Try to incorporate doing "good deeds for the day" every day! You may impact someone else's life in a way that you could not imagine. Tipping a server generously one day may mean that they can pay their phone bill this month. Complimenting a stranger may give them the confidence to apply for their dream job. Reading to a child or volunteering at a school could give an at-risk kid the positive role model that they may not be getting anywhere else. You may not know what influence a simple "good deed" has on someone else, but the impact on that person may be immeasurable.

"If you can dream it, you can do it." ~ Walt Disney

5 WHAT IS HAPPINESS?

"The ancient Greek definition of happiness was the full use of your powers along lines of excellence." ~ *John F. Kennedy*

I think that most of us can agree that happiness comes from feeling that all of our needs are being fulfilled. It can be described as a feeling of satisfaction and contentment. When people have a sense of well-being, it could be said that they have a sense of happiness. When most people are happy, they experience joy. These are positive emotions and experiences, but that does not mean that happy people don't experience negative emotions like sadness, anxiety, or anger. A happy person has better tools and coping mechanisms to deal with those negative emotions when they arise. They may have different ways of processing those emotions that others have not. They may even find meaning in those emotions. Happy people are still going to experience negative emotions, because they are human. They still experience stress, but it is how they handle those stresses that determine their happiness. Most often, instead of seeing stress as resistance, they will look at stress as an opportunity.

Socrates, Plato, and Aristotle

Socrates suggested that to be happy, one must turn their attention away from the body and towards the soul. Self-knowledge, he believed, is the key to finding true happiness. One must be living a life that is right and achieves your deepest good. When we think of the phrase "soul searching", that is indeed to what Socrates was alluding. He believed that reason was the path to a good life, and that one should look inward to find happiness. Happiness is not a given state, but we must make an effort to obtain it.

Plato, a student of Socrates, believed that all human beings naturally desire happiness. He, too, felt that happiness is obtainable with effort and does not depend on material things. He felt happiness and virtue are linked in such a way that you cannot have one without having the other.

An article in Psychology Today read that "the Greeks defined happiness as: 'Happiness is the joy that we feel when we're striving after our potential.'" The Greek word *Eudaimonia* is often translated to mean "happiness". Eudaimonia comes from the words: *Eu* meaning good and *Daimon* meaning soul or self. Greek philosophers derive that Eudaimonia means reaching the best potential for a human being, which includes happiness, virtue, morality, and a meaningful life. It was Aristotle's belief that by working hard, cultivating your virtues, and transcending the slings and arrows that life throws you that you can achieve Eudaimonia. Aristotle believed that a happy life required a broad range of conditions to be met, both physically and mentally.

Aristotle argued that for a happy life, the Mean must be maintained. The Mean is the balance. Similarly, Buddha believed that in order to be happy, you must follow the Middle Path. Likewise, Taoists follow the Way to happiness which requires balance. All of these philosophies encourage the individual to find balance in their lives. They all touch on that happiness is achieved from within.

Hinduism

Hinduism is considered one of the oldest religions of the world, according to many scholars, with its roots going back over 4,000 years. Their beliefs include karma and reincarnation. Suffering is connected to karma, and it is believed to be self-caused. This could be due to karma in this life or in a past life. The Bhagavad Gita is a 700-verse Hindu scripture and within it are several quotes that refer to happiness, including "The key to happiness is the reduction of desires." Others include:

- "It is better to live your own destiny imperfectly than to live an imitation of somebody else's life with perfection."
- "The happiness which comes from long practice, which leads to the end of suffering, which at first is like poison, but at last like nectar - this kind of happiness arises from the serenity of one's own mind."
- "The peace of God is with them whose mind and soul are in harmony, who are free from desire and wrath, who know their own soul."
- "We behold what we are, and we are what we behold."
- "Man is made by his beliefs. As he believes so he is."
- "He who has no attachments can love others, For his love is pure and divine. And it is from those small acts of love you truly can be happy."
- "Free from all thoughts of 'I' and 'mine', man finds absolute peace.
- "There is neither Self-knowledge nor Self-perception to those whose senses are not under control; Without Self-perception, there is no peace and without peace, there can be no happiness."

Buddhism

Buddhism is over 2,500 years old, and its path to happiness is the understanding of suffering. Meditation is a well-known tool used in Buddhism to train the mind to be in the present and not dwell on the past or the future. We are a result of our thoughts. If we think it, we become it. If we think negative thoughts, we become negative. If we think positively, we become positive and happy.

Buddha was born into wealth and privilege, but as a young man, he ventured out into the world and encountered the old, sick, and death that he had been sheltered from all of his life. This made him question his existence, and he then renounced the pleasures of the world. Even though he had chosen to become poor, he was content, because he realized that happiness did not reside in material things. He found a greater meaning in life and a greater purpose. He discovered the "Middle Path" which is moderation.

During meditation, Buddha realized the Four Noble Truths. Life is suffering; we cannot avoid it. From suffering comes cravings, but suffering can be eliminated. And the way of elimination of suffering is through the Eightfold Path, which consists of wisdom, ethical conduct, and mental cultivation.

Along with meditation, mindfulness is an essential practice in Buddhism. It is so important to take the time to "stop and smell the roses". It encourages one to have an awareness of and openness to all the things around us. Buddhists believe that mindfulness can eliminate desires, which can lead to suffering. It can free us from our regrets of the past and obsessive thoughts of the future.

In order to find happiness, Buddha teaches compassion, consideration, love, kindness, and truth. These virtues lead to happiness. Happiness is not just individual, but resides in service to others. We must have the compassion to want happiness for others. He teaches us that we have to let go. Holding on just continues to make you suffer. This could be holding on to a lost love, old clothes, or even ideas that serve no purpose. Also, remember that life is impermanent. We are given a finite period of time on this planet. We need to make each moment count.

Taoism

Taoism is more of a philosophy than a religion, and it is over 2,500 years old. Like Buddhism, Taoist philosophers are believers in living in the moment. When we live too much in the past, it breeds depression. When we focus too much on the future, we are plagued with anxiety. Only by living in the moment will we find happiness. We cannot think of happiness as an end result, but as a process and a lifelong journey. They seek balance in all aspects of their lives. The cornerstone of happiness is balance – everything in moderation.

Taoist practitioners are in touch with nature and its cycles. They attempt to live with nature instead of opposing its natural cycles. For instance, you wouldn't typically plant seeds in the fall. It goes against nature's rhythms. Taoism believes in going with the flow…literally. Instead of paddling against the current, it takes much less effort to go with the flow of water. When you stop consciously pursuing happiness, you will find happiness. In Taoism, contentment equals happiness.

Taoism tries to look at a situation and see if there is a way of avoiding wasting energy and resources to be more effective and efficient. They try to harmonize their minds with the physical world. Meditation and forest bathing are two practices that can help to achieve this balance and harmony. They try to "unlearn". Knowledge and wisdom are not the same thing. Wisdom allows us to throw out what we think that we know in order to adapt to another way of being. This allows us to evolve. Being aware that you don't know anything and being open to knowledge, that is wisdom.

Taoists practitioners learn to be present by removing ourselves from drama. We must drop expectations. Sometimes that best plan is to have no plan. When you surrender to the Way, things work out the way that they are supposed to. You must learn to go with the flow. To be mindful is to become more aware of our environment, and thus, we react intentionally. Do you do things because you are on autopilot or do you take time to be present in the process and act with intention?

In order to be healthy, Taoists believe that we must honor who we are and become in touch with our true nature. We must slow down and take time to observe. We must take our time to mindfully eat. We should observe the rising and falling of our stomach as we inhale and exhale each breath. We must become in tune with our own body rhythms and cycles.

The path of Taoism is to simply accept oneself. One must become in touch with their authentic Self. An easy trap that we fall into is comparing ourselves to others. Marsha has a big house, Larry has a brand new sports car, or Gina just got the promotion that you were wanting. You cannot compare yourself to others for a number of reasons. Primarily, you are on a different journey than someone else. You have a different skill set than others. Secondly, comparing yourself to someone else's successes or gains only creates jealousy and envy. Thirdly, the path that someone else is on might not be right for you. Marsha and Larry might be living beyond their means with the high mortgage and car payments. The position that Gina acquired might have held you back from pursuing a lateral move within the company or kept you from starting your own business. Perspective can change everything. What you may look like as a slight to you or that in some way you are lacking might, in reality, be a blessing to you in disguise. Being critical and judgmental by making comparisons will only move you farther away from your state of "flow". This also ties into the philosophy that you need to let go of things that you have no control over. In other words, shit happens.

So to be happy:
- Happiness must come from within.
- Happiness comes from activity.
- Material things are not necessary for happiness.
- Happiness is living in the now, not the past or future.

In the movie *The Wizard of Oz*, Dorothy traveled far and wide, was poisoned, sent on an impossible mission, and battled a witch. After doing all of that to find her way home, she was made to realize that she had it in her all the time. That is happiness. We may look externally for happiness, but happiness resides within us. Hector in the movie *Hector And The Search For Happiness* comes to the same realization. He is unsatisfied with his job, relationship, and life in general. He sets out to travel the globe to learn what makes other people happy, only to realize that he had everything he needed to be happy all along.

Happiness vs. Pleasure

Some people confuse happiness with pleasure. Pleasure is externally motivated, and it is the gratification that we feel after we have obtained outward desires. It is fleeting. We may find pleasure in food or sex, and while those feelings may be satisfying at the time, they are often short-lived. The seeking of pleasure gives us a good feeling, but can become addictive and have negative long-term consequences. The pursuit of happiness, on the other hand, involves engaging in intentional activities and creating positive habits that have benefits for the long-term. In other words, you cannot find happiness outside of you. You must find it within.

Also, the more you do something that is positive, typically the happier you will be. For example, you may love eating cake, but if you partake in eating cake in excess for a long period of time, even though you may find pleasure in it, your body will become negatively affected by it. However, if you enjoy laughing, you will find that the more that you laugh, the greater the health benefits.

Happiness cannot exist without action. Sitting on the couch watching TV all day doesn't make you happy. You may feel content, but you won't be happy. Happiness lies in the activity of doing what you are passionate about. What makes you feel fulfilled? What brings you joy? What gives you meaning? Happiness is in the connections that you build and relationships that you cultivate. Even if connections have strayed, they can always be rebuilt.

"A journey of a thousand miles must begin with a single step." ~ *Lao Tzu*

6 STRESS MANAGEMENT TECHNIQUES

"Only I can change my life. No one can do it for me." ~ *Carol Burnett*

Stress has become chronic and overwhelming in our daily lives. Since most of us cannot avoid the stress that we are encountering, we must learn to manage it. Many healthcare practitioners and employers are incorporating stress management techniques into their wellness programs. According to the American Institute of Stress, U.S. industry is estimated at a loss of over $300 billion annually as a result of absenteeism, employee turnover, diminished productivity, accidents, medical costs, legal costs, insurance costs, and workers' compensation. Stress is not only killing us, but it's also costing us!

There is a light to this tunnel. There are ways that you can incorporate stress-relieving approaches into your daily life. Try one or all of these techniques and make them habitual. All are beneficial to your health and many can be used complementary to your current medical treatments and therapies. But, of course, these should not be used in lieu of professional medical advice and supervision. And always consult with your physician before you start a new diet plan or exercise program.

You can take a few small steps each day to lead a more stress reduced lifestyle. It is easier to make changes in your life if you take small steps instead of overwhelming yourself. Like in the movie *What About Bob*, you need to take "baby steps" to bring about life changes. The following are methods to incorporate into your life to pursue better physical health, better mental stability, better clarity and focus, better spirituality, and better peace. Your life will be BETTER!

I have an older dog, and when we go for walks, he loves to just sit outside under a tree. If it is a pretty day, we will sit under that tree for about a half an hour or longer. While we sit there, I will sometimes close my eyes and listen to the insects and the birds flying around, smell the air, feel the wind, and enjoy the peace. I will attempt to clear my mind and just enjoy the moment doing nothing but sitting with my dog. He enjoys lying there, looking around. His relaxation rubs off on me. It is a combination of the pinene from the trees that I am breathing in, the taking a break from life for that period of time, and the clearing of my mind and calming of my thoughts. What I just described to you is a combination of forest bathing and meditation with a dash of unplugging from technology.

Diet

"The second day of a diet is always easier than the first. By the second day, you're off it." ~ Jackie Gleason

Diet has become an overused term and one with negative connotations. We hate to use the word "diet". But when using the word "diet" in this book, we will be meaning the food we put into our bodies and the manner in which we prepare it.

In the start of a new year, many people resolve to start a new diet. We say, instead, resolve to eat healthier or make lifestyle changes. A yogic diet, heart-healthy diet, and Mediterranean diet are a balanced combination of:
- **Fruits**
- **Nuts & Legumes**
- **Vegetables**
- **Grains & Pasta**
- **Dairy products**

If you are a carnivore, you are thinking "Where's the beef?" Refraining from meat consumption can be difficult at first, but is beneficial on so many levels. For one, there is the conscious element. Most animals bred for food do not have a pleasant life at all. A lot never see the light of day nor have freedom of movement. You are putting negativity into your body. Second, a vegetarian lifestyle is cheaper. With the growing prices of meat, poultry, and fish, vegetarian choices are more cost-efficient. Thirdly, a vegetarian diet is just healthier. People on a vegetarian or semi-vegetarian diet have lower cholesterol, lower blood pressure, lower stress, and lower rates of heart disease, cancer, and diabetes. "But how will I get enough protein?" Trust me, Americans consume way too much protein. Plus, if you eat cheese, tofu, beans, lentils, yogurt, nuts, and seeds, these are all high in protein. Grab a tablespoon of peanut butter!

There are a plethora of terms of people who limit their meat consumption with a "semi-vegetarian" diet:
- **Flexitarian** - They try to limit their meat intake as much as possible, but occasionally eat meat.
- **Pescatarian** - They restrict their meat consumption to fish and seafood only.

- **Pollotarian** - They restrict their meat eating to poultry and foul.
- **Lacto-ovo vegetarian** - They do not eat meat, but do consume dairy and eggs. This is considered the most common form of vegetarianism.
- **Ovo vegetarian** - They do not eat meat or dairy, but do consume eggs.
- **Lacto vegetarian** - They do not eat meat or eggs, but do consume dairy products such as milk, cheese, and yogurt.
- **Vegan** - These guys are hard-core. They do not consume any animal products or by-products whatsoever.

So don't be scared off by vegetarianism. You don't have to jump feet first in and give up everything all at once. With any kind of change you make, sometimes it is best to take "baby steps". Baby steps often times are the keys to successful transition and change.

How to eat better

Whole, fresh, and unprocessed foods give you energy and strength. When your diet consists of nutritious and sustaining foods, you are on your way to healthy and happy living. Eating organic is healthier because it contains fewer or no pesticides, preservatives, antibiotics, or growth hormones. It is like putting the higher octane gas into your tank.

Also, portion size is important. You don't want to "feel full" when you eat. You want to feel "satisfied". What that means is you don't want to eat so much that you feel miserable and think "I wish I wouldn't have eaten that last bite." You want to have the sensation of wanting more, but not necessarily feeling hungry. This allows your body room to work. If you overeat, your body becomes tired and needs to rest to digest. That slows down your metabolism, and hence, you gain weight. When you finish eating, you should not feel like you need a nap. Also, do not eat at least three hours before you go to bed for this same reason.

Remember, carbs are not the enemy. Lack of exercise and overeating are!

Also, food preparation is very important. The time that you spend, preparing and cooking food can reduce stress. It can also be a form of meditation in and of itself. You are not worrying about your problems or stresses; you are focusing on the tasks at hand of making a meal. This preparation can keep you "in the moment". If you are preparing your meals at home, you are less likely to overeat as most restaurants give much larger portions than the average person needs. If you want to eat out, I would suggest looking at the kids' menu. Most meals on kids' menus are similar to the adult ones, but at much smaller portion sizes. Or when you order, ask the waiter for a to-go box. Once your meal arrives, put half of your meal in the to-go box. It will automatically limit your portion size, and you'll have another meal for later on!

Do not to eat too quickly. You should stay in the moment. Enjoy each bite and take smaller bites. If you take this time to enjoy your food, you are also eating slower which aids in digestion, stress reduction, and reduces overeating.

Foods to avoid or reduce
- Red meat
- Processed foods, junk foods
- Fried foods and overly cooked foods
- White flour and sugar
- Alcohol, tobacco, and caffeine
- Genetically engineered foods
- Eating food too quickly
- Foods with added preservatives, antibiotics, etc.

If you are like me, avoiding at least one of these things is so hard to fathom, let alone accomplish. I have in the past relied on booze to deal with my anxiety, depression, and stress. And while it helped me feel better at the moment, that moment did not last for long. For one, the feeling is fleeting. It does not endure. For another, it can make the depression or anxiety worse after the buzz wears off. And if you had a night of heavy drinking, you may end up wasting the whole next day trying to make yourself feel physically better. And because of that, your depression is increased exponentially. If you have anxiety or panic attacks, those will tend to be more amped up.

Exercise

"Training gives us an outlet for suppressed energies created by stress and thus tones the spirit just as exercise conditions the body." ~ Arnold Schwarzenegger

I know you hear this all the time. Doctors, talk shows, and your super healthy neighbor all preach the same thing. To get healthy, you have to have a proper diet and exercise plan. You hear it all the time, because it's true! No matter how simple it sounds, that's it. Of course, when things sound easy, that doesn't mean that they are. Now, does that mean you shouldn't try? Of course not. The benefits of exercise are countless and proven. Unless your doctor tells you otherwise, exercise is good for everyone.

Should you run out and get a gym membership this January? Not if you aren't going to use it. Making it easy to use is helpful. For instance, if the gym is close to where you live or work, you may be more likely to use it. There are so many gyms out there competing with each other, you can find a good deal on a membership for as low as $10-30 per month. What is your health worth to you? Some insurance companies will give you a discount if you have a gym membership. Some employers will even pay for your gym membership.

"But what if I don't have a gym body?" You shouldn't yet. You are just getting started. Lou Ferrigno wasn't born with huge biceps…hopefully. Everyone starts as a beginner. Don't shame yourself out of making yourself better for you. What is most important is that you stick with it. Lou's body didn't get buff overnight either.

If the gym isn't for you, that's okay, too. There are tons and tons of exercise videos out there, but there is a catch…you have to hit PLAY. It's like the Nike commercial: JUST DO IT! Don't want to do videos? Okay. You can do sit-ups, jumping jacks, and push-ups right in the comfort of your living room. You can even buy exercise equipment for the home, like a treadmill or stationary bike. But don't let them become a clothes hanger! If you are a TV junkie like me, jump on a machine while you are watching your favorite shows on DVR. The time will fly by if you preoccupy yourself and get immersed in the show. You spend hours on the couch watching TV anyway. You can multi-task by watching while peddling. In the time that it takes to watch one sitcom, you will have completed 30-minutes of cardio! Do that five times a week, and see how good you feel at the end of that week. Keep it up for six months, and check out how well your pants fit!

A key to sticking with an exercise regime is to pick activities that you actually enjoy. It won't feel like work if you like doing it. Some people enjoy hiking. Maybe you could take a class. Try tap dancing, karate, kickboxing, CrossFit, or Pilates. There are countless classes to choose from. They will help keep you active as well as give you the social interaction that you may need. Another way of keeping fit and social is to join a team. Do a search for teams in your area to join. There are bowling leagues, kickball teams, softball, flag football, or even cornhole (yes, that's a thing!). Variety in activity will keep you interested.

When considering your potential exercise regime, you should make an effort to combine aerobic conditioning, strength training, and stretching into your plan. Of course, make sure you speak with your physician before incorporating an exercise plan into your life. It is recommended by many physical trainers to include at least thirty minutes of aerobic activity three times a week, strength training such as weights two to three times per week, and stretching at least two to three times per week.

Cardiovascular exercise is key to good health. A minimum of thirty minutes of moderate physical activity can significantly reduce the risk of diabetes, heart disease, and other cardiovascular-related illnesses. It is also important for successful long-term weight loss.

Walking

There are several ways of getting your steps in each day. One way is by simply walking. The average person can burn between 80 to 140 calories per mile walked. The current trend is to try to walk at least 10,000 steps per day to maintain your health. Surprisingly, most people, unless they have an active lifestyle, do not get the needed number of steps per day. The average person takes 2,000 steps for every mile, so if you walk 10,000 steps, you will have walked about five miles. There are several devices on the market now to help you calculate and keep track of your steps. Some of them will even help you track your sleep patterns and heart rate. If you walk 10,000 steps in a day, you will burn between 400-600 calories.

If you have pets, take them on a walk. I'm not talking just having them do their business and coming right back in. I mean a real walk. Walk around the neighborhood for a few blocks (of course, only if you live in a safe area or have a big dog). Your dog needs the exercise just as much as you do, plus the attention that it will get from you with this one-on-one contact. A person of reasonable health should be able to walk for a mile in twenty minutes with no problem, but start off small if that bite seems too big. Start by walking around the block. Tomorrow, add another block. By the end of the week, you could be walking a five-block radius and won't even realize it. Do it before work or at the end of the day after you get home.

Take the time to really look at your neighborhood. Smile and wave at neighbors, then compliment them on their lawn. Check out the blooming flowers, the warm summer breeze, the changing fall colors, or the crisp winter air. This will do two things: give you needed exercise and keep you in the moment. You will find yourself more relaxed, your mind will start to quiet, and your blood pressure will reduce.

Forest Bathing

You don't have to be a serious hiker or cross-country athlete to get the benefit of the outdoors. Many benefits can be found of just being exposed in nature. Forest bathing may sound odd or unheard of to most, but is a great way of reducing stress. Much like sun-bathing, you are exposing yourself to the woods (bathing suit optional). Forest bathing is the Japanese practice called Shinrin-Yoku. Unlike exercise, you are not trying to burn calories doing this. Instead, forest bathing helps you reduce your blood pressure, lower your cholesterol levels, and reduce your heart rate all by just taking a stroll in the woods. For instance, in a three-hour session, you may only walk about a half of a mile or less.

Forest bathing allows you to achieve mindfulness in nature. Some call this Nature Therapy. Whenever our attention is focused on our senses, we are being mindful. We are feeling the grass under our feet and the breeze and sun on our skin. We hear the leaves rustle and birds sing. We smell the pine in the trees and the sweet scent of the flowers. We taste the sweetness of the air on our tongues. We see all the beauty that surrounds us. We are not trying to accomplish anything. We are simply just being in the moment and appreciating what is around us.

There is actually science that backs the benefits of Shinrin-Yoku. There is a substance in the soil that we breathe in when we walk in the woods. It is called *Mycobacterium vaccae*. It is common, harmless, and it makes us feel happier. Evergreens like pines, cedars, and spruces produce phytoncides, which are natural oils within a plant and are part of the tree's defense system to protect it from insects, bacteria, and fungi. They are antibacterial compounds, and they boost the immune system. Phytoncides are composed of terpenes like D-limonene, Alpha-pinene, Beta-Pinene, and Camphene. Dr. Qing Li did a study on these substances and found that phytoncides significantly increased the numbers of NK cells (Natural Killer cells) and NK activity, which work to control viral infections and cancer cells. So get on the fighting side of phytoncides.

According to a 2014 U.N. report, fifty-four percent of the world's population lives in urban areas. Never in our history have more Americans lived in the city than in rural areas. And our health is reflected in that. Environmental Health and Preventative Medicine published a study that showed that people who spent time in the forest had lower cortisol levels, lower blood pressure, and lower pulse rates than those who walked in the city. Studies have even proven that patients who have hospital rooms that face a park or even a tree have a quicker recovery rate than those who do not. Healthcare professionals are beginning to recognize forest bathing as a tool to manage stress. Some hospitals are using forest bathing as a part of their wellness services, such as the Northside Hospital Cancer Institute in Atlanta, Georgia. The positive effects of forest bathing have been exhibited days after the sessions.

Not only are we becoming more urban as a society, but we are also becoming more interior dwelling creatures. Many people are now suffering from vitamin D deficiency. Since we gain more vitamin D from sun exposure than we do food, it is important for us to get outside. Our increased use of sunscreen has also lead to a lack of vitamin D in our bodies. We cover our arms and legs in the colder months and slather on sunscreen in the warmer months. That does not allow our bodies to absorb the sun's ray and get the vitamin D that we so badly need. Of course, I do not suggest rubbing yourselves down with Crisco and bake in the sun, although I do have a cousin that did that. She said it made her tan quicker. We definitely want to avoid getting skin cancer. We need ten to twenty minutes of sun exposure per day without sunscreen to get the amount that our bodies need to convert into vitamin D.

In the winter months especially, we see not only a decrease in vitamin D, but also an increase in Seasonal Affective Disorder, or SAD. Some refer to this as Seasonal Depression. It is a type of depression that is related to the changes in seasons, most often in the winter months when the temperatures are colder, there is less daylight, and there is less time outdoors. Women are diagnosed with SAD four times more often than men. It is believed that people with SAD may produce less vitamin D, and that may play a role in serotonin activity.

Even if you live in the city, you can spend some time in a local park, look at a tree outside your window, or add some plants into your home. Lucky bamboo is an easy plant to take care of, because they only require water and very little sunlight. You can find these bamboo plants in any of your local hardware chains in their garden departments. This plant is not only considered lucky, but it also adds moisture into the air. Another kind of bamboo is the Bamboo Palm, which grows bigger and may require a bit more light. It cleans the air of pollutants. Aloe Vera is also easy to take care of, and its leaves have healing benefits such as having antibacterial and anti-inflammatory properties. It removes formaldehyde from the air.

Yoga
"In yoga, the key to staying youthful is a flexible spine." ~ Mandy Ingber

Yoga and Its Effects on Heart Disease and Stress
The American Heart Association suggests that, for overall cardiovascular health, we get at least 150 minutes of moderately-intensive aerobic activity at least five days per week. Unfortunately, yoga is not considered aerobic activity. However, it is thought that yoga can be used to improve heart health and reduce stress levels, especially as a preventative measure or after facing a cardiac event. Yoga has a plethora of benefits for those that suffer from heart disease. Yoga has been found to lower blood pressure, lower cholesterol, lower heart rate, reduce blood sugar levels, improve respiratory function, increase lung capacity, boost circulation and the immune system, reduces stress, anxiety, and depression, eliminates insomnia, and increase muscle tone and flexibility. It basically improves your overall health.

Aerobic exercise like running or jogging helps improve blood circulation and when done each morning and evening, can burn 600 to 900 calories in a day. A practice of yoga and pranayama after fifteen minutes of cardiovascular exercise can remove heart blockages. Pranayama is effective in improving blood circulation. Just fifteen to twenty minutes of yoga practice can lower stress levels.

What is wonderful about yoga is that anyone can do it, regardless of physical ability or condition, age, or weight. It is also great for people who may have been out of an exercise routine for some time. Of course, you should always discuss any exercise plans with your doctor. Most doctors will recommend more cardiovascular exercises, such as running, jogging, or walking, but the calming effect of yoga is also quite beneficial to the heart patient. Physicians are more readily recommending yoga to their patients as a part of their recovery and rehabilitation program.

Yoga relaxes the mind and the body, which is so important for stress reduction. Stress can have physical effects on the body, including the release of cortisol and adrenaline in the body. Cortisol leads to, among other things, weight gain. Adrenaline can increase blood pressure. Both of these can lead to a narrowing of the arteries. Studies have shown that the circumference of your waistline can be a sign of potential heart issues. One study showed that middle-aged patients who practiced yoga for just three months showed a decrease in the waistline circumference as well as better numbers in their blood work. After a cardiac event, a patient may have increased depression, which yoga can lower instances of this as well.

When faced with issues of the heart, one must look to improving their health with lifestyle changes. Lifestyle changes are crucial in the success of heart patients. Such changes include cessation of smoking and alcohol. Also, being overweight will increase your risk for a heart attack and/or high blood pressure. Losing weight is a must. Exercise is vital in having a healthy heart. It is recommended that one adopt a healthy diet of fruits and green vegetables, which aligns well with a yogic diet. It is also recommended that people get six to eight hours of sleep each night.

Again, exercise is crucial. Getting the heart pumping and toning the muscles are key to improving the health of your heart. Deep breathing temporarily lowers blood pressure and calms the nervous system. Long-term sustained yoga practice is thought to play a role in improving overall health in heart patients. Studies have shown that patients who participated in a twelve-week yoga practice saw an increase in their exercise functionality, and a decrease in their blood pressure and cholesterol levels.

Finding the right teacher/class is essential. For older people or heart patients, a good yoga practice is one that involves not only the postures, but also breathing and meditation. Older people may have issues with their range of motion, arthritis, or osteoporosis that may limit their flexibility. The right instructor will create a safe environment for their students. It is important that the instructor keep the individual student and their needs in mind. These students may need more assistance in modifying poses and may have more limitations than other students. Heart patients also have their limitations in poses that may not be suggested for their situations.

Yoga is beneficial on three levels. The yoga postures work the muscles. Pranayama, or breathing exercises, bring more oxygen into the body. It also reduces blood pressure. Relaxation and meditation calm the nervous system, which in turn, reduces stress.

There are a number of yoga postures that are beneficial for heart patients. If one has experienced a heart attack, Reclining Bound Angle Pose (Supta Baddhakonasana), Reclining Hero Pose (Supta Virasana), Bridge Pose (Setubandha Sarvangasana), Supported

Headstand (Salamba Sirsasana), Upward Facing Two-Foot Staff Pose (Viparita Dandasana), Camel Pose (Ustrasana), Legs-Up-The-Wall Pose (Viparita Karani), Corpse Pose (Savasana), and Ujjayi Pranayama are suggested postures. There are a number of postures that benefit high blood pressure, such as Standing Forward Bend (Uttanasana), Downward Facing Dog (Adhomukha Svanasana), Hero Pose (Virasana), Wide-Angle Seated Forward Bend Pose (Upavista Konasana), Bound Angle Pose (Baddhakonasana), Forward Facing Hero Pose (Adhomukha Virasana), Reclining Hand-to-Big-Toe Pose (Supta Padangusthasana), Reclining Bound Angle Pose (Supta Baddhakonasana), Reclining Hero Pose (Supta Virasana), Plow Pose (Halasana), Bridge Pose (Setubandha Sarvangasana), the Auspicious Pose (Swastikasana), Legs-Up-the-Wall Pose (Viparita Karani), Corpse Pose (Savasana), Ujjayi Pranayama, and Viloma 2 Pranayama. Some of these poses help to strengthen the heart and also add flexibility to the body.

In a study published in *Medicine & Science in Sports & Exercise*, patients were measured for endurance, flexibility, inflammation, and quality of life. Patients were placed into two groups, with one group practicing yoga for six to eight weeks. At the conclusion of the study, both groups were measured and discovered significant improvements in the group that participated in yoga. Improvement was found in not just one area, but across the board.

Pranayama also has great benefits for the heart patient. This breathing technique can remove toxins from the body and give positive energy. It improves blood circulation, removes blockages in the arteries, releases stress, reduces depression and anxiety, and calms the mind and body. Pranayama is easy to do and can be done just about anywhere, whether laying down, sitting, or even walking. One study says that heart patients who followed a yoga practice that included pranayama for thirty days showed significant improvement in heart function.

Meditation has been found to reduce the likeliness of heart attacks and strokes. Several studies have shown that regular meditation can help lower blood pressure and reduce anxiety and depression. The National Institute of Health discovered that heart patients who regularly meditate can reduce their risk of heart attack or stroke by nearly fifty percent. Another study followed 201 African-Americans who were at a higher risk for heart disease. They were asked to either follow a diet and exercise plan or practice meditation. After about five years, the researchers found a reduction in the overall risk of heart attack, stroke, and death in the meditation group by about forty-eight percent.

Meditation reduces cortisol levels in the blood, as well as triggers the brain into releasing dopamine and oxytocin. People who practice meditation are significantly less likely to have another heart attack within five years. Those who meditate regularly feel more balanced and less stressed. Stanford University did a study where people who participated in an eight-week mindfulness course had an increase in the activity in the areas of the prefrontal cortex. That is the area of the brain that regulates emotions, which in turn, reduces stress.

This is not to say that yoga can replace conventional medicine, but rather it is a wonderful complement to it. Yoga can also reduce the side effects of some medications. In order to successfully prevent or recover from heart disease, lifestyle changes must be made. Medication, diet, and exercise are of the utmost of importance, and yoga can play a significant role in improving the prognosis of heart disease. These steps can prolong life and even reverse heart disease.

Yoga Practice

The great thing about Yoga is that ANYONE can do it. You don't have to be sweating in a 90-degree room or be a circus contortionist to do yoga. Yoga can be as simple or complicated as you want it to be. Yoga can be basic stretching exercises done from the comfort of a stable chair or on the floor. It can be done in your living room, in your back yard, on a beach, at a park, well, the options are endless. No expensive equipment is required, but you can use props such as Bolsters, Blocks, Blankets, or Belts to help support you in poses. (I call those the 4 B's.)

Yoga is more than just exercises. Yoga is a collection of techniques and practices that aims to integrate the mind, body, and spirit. The goal is to achieve a state of enlightenment or oneness with the Universe.

There are five paths of Yoga:
- Hatha
- Tantra
- Raja
- Jnana
- Bhakti

Hatha attempts to achieve unity of the mind, body, and spirit through the practice of Asanas (poses), Pranayama (breathing), Mudra (body gestures), and Shatkarma (internal cleansing).

Tantra Yoga is often associated with sex, and it is to a point. But Tantra Yoga focuses on using the body as a temple of worship. It combines Asana, Mantra, Mudra, Bandha, and Chakra work.

Raja Yoga is oneness through meditation. It deals with the mastery of the mind.

Jnana Yoga is the yoga of wisdom. The goal is to become liberated from thoughts and perceptions and to achieve a union in the inner Self.

Bhakti Yoga is the yoga of devotion. Swami Sivananda writes, "Bhakti softens the heart and removes jealousy, hatred, lust, anger, egoism, pride, and arrogance. It infuses joy, divine ecstasy, bliss, peace, and knowledge. All cares, worries and anxieties, fears, mental torments, and tribulations entirely vanish. The devotee is freed from the Samsaric wheel of births and deaths. He attains the immortal abode of everlasting peace, bliss, and knowledge".

There are nine limbs of Devotion: listening to scriptures, singing devotional songs, remembering the Divine, selfless service, ritual worship, prostration before the image of one's chosen representation of the Divine, serving without ego, friendship with the Divine, and complete surrender of the self to the Divine.

Hatha develops a strong and flexible body. Raja creates a disciplined and concentrated mind. Jnana cultivates a keen intellect. Bhakti brings about an open and loving heart.

There are eight limbs of yoga:
- Yama
- Niyama
- Asana
- Pranayama
- Pratyahara
- Dharana
- Dhyana
- Samadhi

Yama has to do with the ethics of yoga. Niyama deals with self-discipline and spiritual observances. Think of it as Yamas are things you shouldn't do, and Niyamas are things to do. Together, they form your morals and a common code of conduct. They are the map for your life's journey.

Asanas are the physical exercises that most people think of when they hear the word Yoga. These postures keep the body strong, flexible, and relaxed.

Pranayama is your breath control. It recognizes the connection of breath with the mind and emotions.

Pranayama helps you move from pose to pose. Prana means life force.

Pratyahara represents the withdrawal or sensory transcendence. This is where we attempt to detach from our senses and draw our awareness away from the external world. We turn our attention inwardly. Think of it as stepping back and taking a good look at yourself in the mirror. It draws your attention toward silence rather than toward things.

Dharana is the process of dealing with these outside distractions. It is the practice of concentration, or focusing on a single, mental object. Dhyana is the practice of meditation.

Finally, the eighth limb is Samadhi, the state of ecstasy. At this stage, you transcend the Self altogether. You realize the connection with the Divine. This is your connection with all living things. You have the peace of all understanding. This is the ultimate goal: joy, fulfillment, and freedom.

Props Usage and Restorative Yoga

Restorative yoga helps heal the mind and the body. It can reduce fatigue and stress, and help you relax. It also reduces anxiety and depression. Restorative yoga increases strength and flexibility.

Yoga postures can be divided into seven categories: Standing Asanas, Sitting Asanas, Forward Bends, Twists, Inversions, Back Bends, and Reclining Asanas. Props are useful in aiding the practitioner in supporting the body during stretching and relaxing. This allows one to hold the poses for a longer period of time. It also allows one to open the body through passive stretching.

Props that can be used in Restorative yoga include: bolsters, blankets (folded or rolled), foam and wooden blocks, chairs, high stools, low open stools, wooden benches, half-halasana stools, mats, yoga belts, and crepe bandages. Each prop has a specific function in Restorative yoga which allows the person to go into the pose deeper and have more of an impact.

Yoga mats are good for carpet-areas, but can also be used on wood floors. They provide a clean space, but you may want to make sure that the mat is a sticky one to avoid slipping of the feet and hands. That could cause injury, and the purpose of props is to avoid any injury.

Bolsters can be used to open up the chest and abdomen. When placed under the back, shoulders, and head, they can lengthen the spine and open the chest. They may be used to correct posture.

A yoga strap can provide support and leverage. It can be an extension of the arms. A strap can help support your leg in the Tree Pose.

Blocks are used to take the strain out of poses, relieve muscle tension, to support parts of the body, and to aid in balancing and alignment. Blocks can be placed under the palms during Downward-Facing Dog to allow the heels to rest flat on the floor, takes the pressure off the shoulders, and gives more length to the spine. Blocks give great support during Triangle and Half-Moon

Poses.

Blankets can serve many purposes. They provide support and cushioning in several poses. They can be used to create a comfortable, yet firm seat for meditation. Folded and rolled blankets give great support during backbends, as do bolsters and blocks.

Metal chairs are also useful in many postures. One can fold themselves over the back of the chair to form a more passive Downward-Facing Dog. One may rest their head on the seat of the chair during forward bends. Chairs also help with backbends.

Even a wall can be used as a prop. One may press your palms into a wall while doing forward bends to add support for tight hamstrings. A wall can give good support during headstands and other inversions.

There are countless ways to incorporate props into your practice. Using them will grant you the ability to get into postures that you may not be able to otherwise and for longer periods of time. They allow the body to relax while being supported. They allow students who may be apprehensive toward yoga to participate and thrive. These are just a few of the reasons that I was drawn to Restorative Yoga.

Meditation

"When you're a kid, you lay in the grass and watch the clouds going over, and you literally don't have a thought in your mind. It's purely meditation, and we lose that." ~ *Dick Van Dyke*

Meditation is a practice of training your mind. Just as you can train your body through physical exercises, you can train your mind with meditation. What you are trying to do is "empty" your mind. You may think, *"Oh, sitting and thinking about nothing? That's easy."* It's not as easy as you think.

First, sit or lay down in a relaxed position. Use your breathing exercises to relax your body and calm your mind. Focus on your breath. Notice how your belly rises and falls with each breath. As thoughts creep into your mind, don't get frustrated, but rather acknowledge the thought, and then let it slip away. When you begin, you will notice that it is quite difficult to "not think". Try doing this for just a few minutes each day. Some days will be more difficult than others, but each week, add a few more minutes. Before you know it, you may be doing it for twenty minutes.

What is the point? The point is to make your mind calm, focused, and peaceful. The more calm and peaceful your mind is, the happier you will be. The more focused you become, the more productive you will be. Once you are more peaceful, you become more appreciative, compassionate, and kind. Like with breathing exercises, meditation will help you relax, relieve stress, energize yourself, along with other numerous other physical and psychological benefits. Meditation will help change your mind. Studies using an fMRI to scan the brain while people chanted have shown that chanting the word "om" could engage the area of the brain that is associated with inner peace and calmness. You will learn a lot about yourself. You will notice that your thoughts will transform from negative to positive over time.

Take a clean glass and scoop it into a puddle of muddy water. At first, one can observe the sediment swirling around the glass. It is impossible to see through the glass for the thickness of the muck. But given time, once the glass is still and the sediment falls to the bottom of the glass, the water becomes clear. This is an analogy for the mind. Thoughts tumble around like the sediment in the glass and cloudy our minds. If we can still our thoughts, our minds can become clear.

Relaxation

Relaxation may not be the goal of meditation, but it certainly is often the result. When you are relaxed, your body reaps the benefits with lower blood pressure and heart rate, improved circulation, and lower anxiety and stress. On a spiritual level, the ultimate benefit of meditation is freeing the mind from attachments, or enlightenment. Buddhists believe it creates a calmness of the mind and balance.

How to meditate

Meditation can be as simple as sitting with your spine straight or lying down in a comfortable position, closing your eyes, breathing naturally, and focusing your attention on your breath. You can start by just trying to do this for five minutes. See how you do.

There are several tools that you can use during your meditation practice to help you concentrate.
- Music
- Candle staring
- Repeating a mantra
- Visualizations

Try doing your meditation practice every day, even if it is only for a few minutes. It is also a good idea to pick a certain part of the day to practice so that it is easier to create a routine. It is recommended to practice meditation early in the morning or at dusk, which is the peak of your energies. An early morning session can get your day off to a great start or a dusk session can help you wind down and reflect as your day ends. But there is no right or wrong time. Any time that you can fit it in can be beneficial to you.

Tai Chi & Qi Gong

These are ancient Chinese practices that combine slow, deliberate movements, meditation, and breathing exercises. Tai Chi and Qi Gong are forms of martial arts that can help your circulation, balance, and alignment. Chi or Qi (both pronounced "chee") literally means "energy" or "life force". They are low-impact moving meditations that involve standing and balancing. They can be done at any physical level and at any age. They are excellent physical activities for beginners as well as people with health conditions. Anyone can benefit from it. The intensity is low, so the impact on your joints and muscles is minimal. You will flow from position to position and do so in beautiful movements. Tai Chi and Qi Gong can be done indoors and outdoors. Comfortable shoes and loose clothes are a must. Otherwise, there is nothing else you need to do it.

Tai Chi began over 500 years ago in China and has been described as the Perfect Exercise and as "Meditation in Motion". This mind-body practice has been found to benefit in treating and preventing many health issues.

Most of you are familiar with the Yin-Yang symbol, which is a symbol identified with Tai Chi and with Taoism. It represents opposing elements that need to be kept in harmony and balance. The Yin-Yang symbolizes the balance between energies. Tai chi is thought to aid in promoting this balance.

Benefits of Tai Chi:
- Improves balance and flexibility
- Reduces pain and inflammation
- Reduces stress, anxiety, and depression
- Increases energy and stamina
- Increases muscle strength
- Lowers blood pressure and improves heart health
- Enhances the immune system
- Promotes better sleep quality
- Improved gait and posture in patients of Parkinson's disease
- Relief in joint pain in patients with Fibromyalgia
- Improved blood glucose levels in patients with type 2 diabetes

Reiki

Reiki is a Japanese spiritual healing art that comes from the word Rei, meaning "Universal Life" and Ki, meaning "Energy". It was developed in 1922 by Japanese Buddhist Mikao Usui, but it is not affiliated with any religion. This life energy flows through all living things. Reiki is a technique of reducing stress and increasing relaxation. A Reiki Practitioner will basically be "laying on hands", in which the practitioner places their hands lightly on or over the person's body. Reiki is a simple and natural method of spiritual healing.

Reiki is not a cure for an illness, but rather assists the body in facilitating healing. It is a wonderful complement to traditional medicine and has been practiced in hospitals and medical facilities.

Benefits:
- Reduces stress
- Promotes relaxation
- Reduces depression and anxiety
- Increases mobility
- Heals infections and inflammation
- Aids symptoms associated with cancer
- Enables emotional clarity and spiritual growth
- Facilitates inner peace and harmony
- Helps relieve pain from migraine, arthritis, and sciatica

Does it work? In short, yes, if you want it to. It is hard for Westerners to wrap their minds around Reiki, because it is difficult to measure. We are so used to popping pills and getting injections that we are skeptical of things that cannot easily be measured. While some critics claim a placebo effect, you cannot discount the patients' results. As a patient, you must be open to alternative therapies for them to really work for you. No negative Nancys. There have been studies done to show reductions in stress and fatigue in patients after sessions.

Touch is powerful! Our skin is the largest organ of our bodies. Has a pat on the back or a hug ever made you feel better? You bet it did! Touch is fundamental to the human experience. Conversely, a lack of physical connection is detrimental to our health. Studies have proven that infants that experienced touch, were held, and were stroked developed stronger immune systems than those who did not. Premature infants who received three 15-minute sessions of touch therapy each day for five to ten consecutive days gained forty-seven percent more weight than those who received only standard medical care. Research has also shown that kids that experienced greater physical affection during childhood had lower rates of adult physical violence. Touch reduces stress, lowers blood pressure, and lowers cortisol. Patients with Alzheimer's showed a reduction in stress and depression.

"Energy cannot be created or destroyed; it can only be changed from one form to another." ~ Albert Einstein

Laughter is the best medicine!

"Laughter is the tonic, the relief, the surcease for pain." ~ Charlie Chaplin

The benefits of laughter to the human body are nearly immeasurable. There are quite complex and sophisticated physiological reactions that happen when we laugh. Our bodies respond to these reactions in several ways. Firstly, there is a decrease in stress hormones, such as cortisol and adrenaline, as well as an increase in beta-endorphins (which lower feelings of depression), when we laugh. Your body responds to laughter even if it is self-induced, or forced, laughter. Laughter also prompts the body to produce more T-cells, which boost our immune systems. People who laugh more tend to live longer and tend to be healthier overall.

Humor is a great functioning tool to use against stress. It can be a self-defense mechanism. It's like the old saying "Laugh or cry"; in most situations, those are your two options. If you can laugh at your misfortune, it has no control over you.

Laughter is the best medicine. It:
- Relaxes the whole body
- Boosts the immune system
- Triggers the release of endorphins
- Improves the function of the heart
- Burns calories (Laughing for 10-15 minutes can burn 40 calories!)
- Decreases pain

And that's just the physical stuff. Laughter also:
- Eases anxiety and depression
- Relieves stress
- Improves your mood
- Improves self-esteem
- Alleviates anger and frustration
- Strengthens relationships and reduces loneliness
- Enhances teamwork and helps defuse conflict
- Just makes us more attractive!

There is a strong link between laughter and mental health. Why do you think sitcoms and comedies are so popular?

Great. How do I start? Start by simply **smiling**. Smiling will make you physically feel better. According to Scientific American, making an emotional face influences your feelings. Charles Darwin wrote that "the free expression by outward signs of an emotion intensifies it."

- **Smile**. When you walk down the street or hall, make eye contact and smile at those you pass. Say hello. Now, if

you live in big cities, people may not know how to take it, but give it a try. You will eventually find this has an effect on others.
- **Count your blessings.** That's another old saying, but it works. Take the time to literally make a list of the good things in your life. People focus so much on what's wrong, you'll be surprised how grateful you will feel when you see in black and white what is so right!
- **Surround yourself with fun people.** They always say if you want to be successful, surround yourself with successful people. The same can be said for happiness.

Take your inner child on a play date! Create opportunities to laugh:
- Watch a funny TV show or movie
- Read the comics
- Share a joke
- Play with a pet
- Play with children
- Don't be afraid to be silly
- Go to a comedy club or Improv theater
- Have a game night with friends
- Go out bowling, karaoke, putt-putt, or any fun activity
- Go to a "Laughter" class

CAUTION: Laughter can be highly contagious.
WARNING: 5 out of 5 doctors will eventually die.

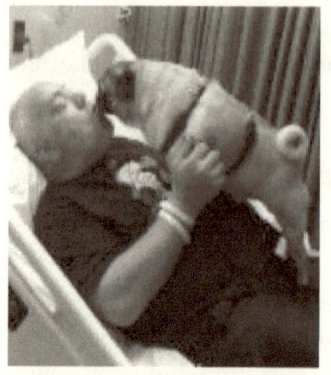
Randy Alexander and Rufus

Christy and Roscoe

Freddie

Want more laughter in your life? Get a pet. Not only will you receive a companion for life, but you will also receive unconditional love. Studies have shown that pets reduce your stress, decrease depression, lower blood pressure, and so much more.

Aromatherapy

"It's so nice to get flowers while you can still smell the fragrance." ~ Lena Horne

Aromatherapy and Its Effects on Heart Disease and

Stress

Aromatherapy is the use of plant substances to benefit good health and well-being. These plant substances have been extracted into the form of essential oils. These oils can be extracted in a number of ways, including steam distillation, hydro-diffusion, solvent extraction, CO2 extractions, cold pressing, or enfleurage. Various parts of the plant are used for extraction: fruit, flowers, leaves, grasses, bark, roots, needles, and resins. Essential oils have been found to have a positive effect on major systems of the body, including the respiratory, digestive, cardiovascular, endocrine, muscular, skeletal, and lymphatic. The oils are often inhaled, used topically, and sometimes ingested.

Aromatherapy has been traced back to possibly the earliest stages of humanity, possibly over 10,000 years ago. Essential oils have been used in various cultures including India, China, Egypt, Greece, Rome, and the Mediterranean. The term "aromatherapy" has been only used since around the 1930s. Egyptians used essential oils in embalming to inhibit bacteria and reduce decomposition of the body's tissues. Hippocrates, the "Father of Medicine", used aromatics to combat the plague and to treat female complaints and disorders.

You can use essential oils in your hair, facial scrubs, facial oils or creams, as a personal scent or mist, on a loofah, in shampoos and conditioners, body and massage oils, or in a compress or linament.

Aromatherapy and the use of essential oils can reduce stress as well as aid in improving and preventing heart disease. A study published in the European Journal of Preventative Cardiology found that aromatherapy is beneficial in reducing stress.

There are a number of essential oils that can be recommended for **heart disease**, including: Cypress (*Cupressus sempervirens*),

Ylang Ylang (*Cananga odorata*), Marjoram (*Origanum majorana*), Clary Sage (*Salvia sclarea*), and Geranium (*Pelargonium graveolens*). Essential oils such as Marjoram (*Origanum majorana*), Ylang Ylang (*Cananga odorata*), Helichrysum (*Helichrysum italicum*), and Lemon (*Citrus limon*) are recommended for high blood pressure. Lemongrass (*Cymbopogon flexuosus*), Cinnamon (*Cinnamomum zeylanicum*), and Lemon (*Citrus limon*) have been used to reduce high cholesterol. Now, it is crucial to make sure that before you use ANY essential oil or other therapies that there are no contradictions to medications as well as to other health issues. For instance, if you have trouble sleeping, you will want to make sure that you are not taking a stimulating substance close to bedtime.

Aromatherapy has not been a widely accepted form of therapy in the eyes of the medical community due to the lack of conclusive evidence. According to Healthline.com, "Aromatherapy using essential oils can help lower anxiety and blood pressure, but only in short bursts. Longer exposure can have the opposite effect." While researchers feel that there is no conclusive evidence that aromatherapy has therapeutic effects on heart disease, there is some evidence that aromatherapy can lower stress and anxiety, which are contributing risk factors for high blood pressure and heart disease. Some research has shown that aromatherapy is not helpful for long periods (over two hours).

Another research study in Taiwan conducted an experiment on prolonged exposure to essential oil vapors. They used vaporizers with Bergamot (*Citrus bergamia*) oil, and tested the blood pressure of 100 young spa workers that stayed in the room for two hours. Their blood pressure was tested every fifteen minutes. According to the European Journal of Preventative Cardiology, Nov. 29, 2012, "For the first hour that the study volunteers stayed in the room, their heart rates and blood pressures dropped slightly. But after 75 minutes, the trend reversed. Heart rates and blood pressures began to climb. Average increases were very small, about two points for systolic blood pressure -- the top number -- and about two beats per minutes for heart rate."

Another research clinical trial was performed to test the effect of aromatherapy on the quality of sleep in heart disease patients hospitalized in intensive care units of hospitals of the Isfahan University of Medical Science in 2010, where 64 patients in CCU were given trials. The intervention included three nights, each time nine hours of aromatherapy with lavender (*Lavandula angustifolia*) oil for the experimental group, while the controlled groups received no aromatherapy. The results of this study showed that of the sleep quality in the two groups, the group that received the lavender (*Lavandula angustifolia*) oil experiment showed significant improvement. The study, therefore, suggested that using aromatherapy can improve the quality of their sleep and health.

In a similar study designed to assess the effect of lavender (*Lavandula angustifolia*), Roman chamomile (*Chamaemelum nobile*), and neroli (*Citrus aurantium*) oil blend on anxiety, sleep, and blood pressure in coronary artery disease patients after a stent insertion who were admitted to the ICU. Between August 1, 2010, to November 20, 2010, patients were admitted to the cardiovascular ICU at the Eulji University Hospital in Daejeon, Korea. In this study, they used Lavender (*Lavandula angustifolia*) to suppress heart stimulation and lower blood pressure. Chamomile (*Chamaemelum nobile*), due to its calming effect, was used to relieve the anxiety and stress. Neroli (*Citrus aurantium*) was found to be effective in reducing insomnia also due to its calming effect. The method of application that they used was inhalation of the essential oil blend.

Lavender (*Lavandula angustifolia*) has been well-known for its calming properties. According to Dr. Eric Zielinski, "Scientists discovered that lavender essential oil treatment helped induce a decrease in oxidative stress, which is known to cause heart disease..." Rosemary (*Rosmarinus officinalis*) has been found to have the ability to normalize blood pressure. Other studies have revealed that bergamot (*Citrus bergamia*) essential oil reduces high blood pressure when it is diffused and inhaled for fifteen to sixty minutes. Those who inhaled this essential oil had a reduction in their anxiety level as well as an improved mood. Even Vanderbilt University and Medical Center are using essential oils to reduce workplace stress. Ylang ylang (*Cananga odorata*) has been used to balance heart function. Marjoram (*Origanum majorana*) helps smooth heart muscle tissue. Cypress (*Cupressus sempervirens*) has been found to improve circulation and lymphatic drainage. Helichrysum (*Helichrysum italicum*) is known to improve circulation and reduce blood viscosity.

After the experiment, the anxiety levels in the aromatherapy group had a significant reduction compared to the control group. Also, there was a significant difference in the sleep score between the aromatherapy group and the controlled group. As for blood pressure, the aromatherapy group had more stabilized blood pressure use. According to the Korea Institute of Oriental Medicine, "The aromatherapy had a positive effect on reducing anxiety, increasing sleep, and stabilizing BP in the patients in the cardiovascular ICU after cardiac stent insertion; therefore, it may be used as an independent nursing intervention." The discussion of the study went on to state, "In summary, aromatherapy reduced anxiety, increased sleep, and stabilized the BP of patients undergoing cardiac stent insertion. Among alternative therapies that have recently been introduced, aromatherapy is easy to apply, fast-acting and can be used in independent nursing interventions. More research is necessary for it to become a suitable nursing intervention in practice."

Those are three separate studies that show varying results. But two of the three tests showed positive results from the use of aromatherapy. The first did show positive results as well, but to a point. After one hour, the positive effects were lost.

Regardless, with stress being such a crucial risk factor for heart disease, aromatherapy warrants further acknowledgment to its beneficial attributes. Rose (*Rosa damascena*), clary sage (*Salvia sclarea*), cypress (*Cupressus sempervirens*), chamomile (*Chamaemelum nobile*), howood (*Cinnamomum camphora var linalool*), juniper (*Juniperus communis*), marjoram (*Origanum majorana*), melissa (*Melissa officinalis*), cedar (*Cedrus atlantica*), frankincense (*Boswellia frereana*), helichrysum (*Helichrysum italicum*), myrrh (*Commiphora myrrha*), neroli (*Citrus aurantium*), ylang ylang (*Cananga odorata*), lavender (*Lavandula angustifolia*), bergamot (*Citrus bergamia*), orange (*Citrus sinensis*), and lemon (*Citrus limon*) are examples of essential aromatic oils that are commonly used to **relieve stress**. These essential oils have also been shown to aid in **lowering blood pressure**.

But with the essential oils, there may be precautions that you must take into consideration. For instance, if the client is pregnant, it is best to avoid oils such as Cedar (*Cedrus atlantica*), Clary sage (*Salvia sclarea*), or Cypress (*Cupressus sempervirens*). Clary sage (*Salvia sclarea*) also can create a drunken effect when taken with alcohol. Chamomile (*Chamaelmelum nobile*) may cause sensitivity in those who have ragweed allergies. It should also be avoided for those in the first trimester of pregnancy. It also has a calming effect, so it would be good to take around bedtime. Lemon (*citrus limon*) is stimulating in nature, so you should not use it four to six hours before bedtime. There is the possibility of it being phototoxic, so do not use it in a bath. Sweet orange (*Citrus sinensis*) may cause dermal irritation and is not advised for use in a bath. It is also phototoxic. Rose (*Rosa damascena*) is a very strong oil, so proper dilution is important. Ylang ylang (*Cananga odorata*) should be avoided with hypersensitive, diseased, or damaged skin. Overuse may result in lightheadedness, headaches, or nausea.

A blended oil may be quite appropriate for heart patients. I would suggest a possible combination of Lemon (*citrus limon*) or Orange (*Citrus sinensis*) (**Top Notes**) with Lavender (*Lavandula angustifolia*) or Chamomile (*Chamaelmelum nobile*) (**Middle Notes**) and Rose (*Rosa damascena*) or Neroli (*Citrus aurantium*) (**Base Notes**). These combinations are beneficial for high blood pressure, poor circulation, and stress. These also have minimal precautions for this type of client.

In conclusion, like with most things, I would say use in moderation. Although the medical community may be apprehensive due to lack of sufficient research and evidence, I do think that there is enough positive evidence available to support the use of aromatherapy for aiding health issues such as heart disease, reducing high blood pressure, and stress relief.

Herbalism

Herbalism is the study, cultivation, harvesting, and utilization of herbs, for medicinal, aromatherapy, and culinary purposes. It is an ancient practice that goes back thousands of years. Evidence of plants being used medicinally dates back to the Paleolithic era. Egyptians used herbs in embalming their dead, and illustrations have been depicted in tombs. Jars were even found to have trace amounts of herbs contained within them. Greeks, Romans, and Chinese all have a vast history of their uses of herbal medicine.

Plants have been used as the basis for treatment throughout most of human history, and some of our modern medicines are based on herbal remedies.

In some areas of the world, herbs are most people's main source of medicine. They not only are used to aid in ailments, but also used as supplements as a preventative measure. Herbal medicine can be administered in a number of ways, including: teas, infusions, decoctions, tinctures, bolus, douche, enema, inhalation, liniments, oils, poultices, salves, and syrups.

Care must be taken when harvesting these herbs. A study of the environment is crucial. It is important not to waste or overuse endangered plants. It is essential to replenish stocks. The parts of the plants that are used include the roots, barks, leaves, seeds, and flowers.

It is also important to know the precautions of herbs and be aware of any interactions and contradictions. For instance, certain herbs are not recommended for pregnant women or children of a certain age. It is very important to be able to accurately identify herbs to avoid accidentally using herbs that might be threatening or dangerous.

Standardization is not mandated in the United States. It is important to know the sources and purity of the herbs that you use. Labels on herbal supplements are not always accurate as to the amount of the herb that it contains, and sometimes, there is no trace of that herb at all. This can be potentially harmful.

Herbalists must know how to wildcraft or cultivate herbs, diagnose possible conditions, come up with a treatment plan, and prepare herbal medications.

Journaling

"I started writing a journal, and I was learning so much along the way. How to deal with your family, how to deal with your friends." ~ Tom Brokaw

Another way to deal with stress is by journaling. It's not just for teenage girls. You can vent your thoughts through the written word by releasing pent-up feelings and thoughts. In addition to helping you reduce stress, it can also sharpen your memory, boost your mood, and strengthen your emotional functions. Some studies even suggest that journaling can strengthen and improve the immune system. It enhances your communications skills, both verbally and written, as well as your reading skills. It can help you set and meet goals. Journaling can also improve your quality of life.

Journaling can reduce stress, and it is proven. Even just journaling a few times a month can lower your blood pressure and improve liver functionality. Also, journaling before bedtime can help you develop better sleep habits. It is an effective tool to help you clear your head as well as make connections between your thoughts and feelings. It requires you to apply the analytical part of your brain at the same time while giving your brain the freedom of creativity. Both the left and right brain are being used simultaneously.

The art of journaling keeps your brain on its toes. It helps to boost your memory and comprehension while also increasing your memory capacity, which may reflect in improved cognitive processing. It can improve your mood. In the long-run, journaling can give you a sense of overall well-being and happiness. By keeping tabs on your feelings and even physicality, you become more in tune with your overall health as well as inner needs and wants. Journaling can also be quite cathartic. It can help you identify patterns in your life. It is a great tool to help not only manage stress, but also anxiety and depression.

Journaling has been found to be quite helpful for those with Post Traumatic Stress Disorder (PTSD) or other trauma issues. It allows us to confront inhibited emotions and process difficult events. It guides us to compose a narrative about past events and experiences. We then become more self-aware and detect unhealthy patterns of behavior. It gives us the freedom to take control of our lives. People with obsessive disorders or eating disorders can find journaling beneficial by encouraging them to confront their issues and prevent them from distancing themselves from these issues. This, in turn, helps them to properly manage their emotions and cope with the stress. If you have lost a loved one, journaling can help you to process your grief and reduce the more severe symptoms of the bereavement. If your issue is one of addiction, writing in a recovery journal can aid you in recording your struggles as well as your accomplishments.

Seeing what you have accomplished on paper is quite powerful. Each year, I make a list of the accomplishments that I have made that year. It prevents me from beating myself up for the perceived things that I have not done, and it gives me a sense of motivation and gratitude. It prepares me for the upcoming year by getting my mind prepared to set goals. It sets up a more positive perspective of your current life and provides the drive for the future without becoming overwhelmed.

Try writing about gratitude. Write down the things that you are grateful for every day. There is always something to be grateful for. Regularly journaling about the positive things in your life can improve your disposition and prepare you to better deal with the rough patches in life when they occur. It can give you a better perspective on what is really important to you and help you truly appreciate your life. You will discover what really matters to you, what you need, and what you can live without.

You don't have to start out with any huge revelations. You can start by writing just one little line. Write about what you ate for lunch. It can be purely a stream of consciousness. You don't have to be a good writer. Just write something. And journaling is easy and cheap. You can buy a basic composition book for less than a dollar. The hardest part is the start. Like Nike says, just do it! Write first thing in the morning when you first wake up, or write before you go to bed. Once you get in the habit, the words will flow out of you like a stream after a spring rain.

You can express your deepest thoughts and feelings without fear of judgment or shame. When you journal, be mindful of when negative thoughts creep in. Replace those negative thoughts with positive self-talk. You must remember to be kind to yourself. It is okay to release your negativity through your journal, but try to keep the focus on your positives. You want to shift from a negative mindset to a more positive one.

Unplug

"Technology is a useful servant but a dangerous master." ~ *Christian Lous Lange*

With social media being so predominant in today's society, we are constantly on our phones, tablets, and laptops, scrolling through our feeds. If we aren't doing that, we are playing video games and watching TV. Technology has opened us up to more information than no other generation before us. But all of this freedom has made us quite closed off. We have created our own little prisons via Facebook and Twitter. We spend countless hours checking our phones and updating our statuses. This is time that could have been better spent working on projects, focusing on our goals, reading a book, or even communicating with real people!

And we spend all of this time on social media with people we barely know or barely even like. We are missing out on real human connections. We have lost the art of personal communication. Try talking to a millennial today. They don't know how to make eye contact when they talk IRL (in real life). Don't get me started on people who don't know how to give a proper handshake! In many urban areas, if you try to make casual conversation with someone, they think you are trying to mug them. Humans are naturally social creatures. Most people need to have human contact in order to survive. Socialization is as crucial to human endurance as water, food, and shelter.

It is also important to have a strong support system. In regards to stress, it is important to be able to have someone to lean on. Being able to share your thoughts and concerns with someone else is a great way of alleviating the burden on your shoulders. Just having someone to bounce ideas off, someone to vent to, or someone to cheer you up can take away some of the excessive stress that we encounter daily. Just knowing that someone has your back can help your disposition so much. Also, the give and take of a relationship allows your compassion, gratitude, and understanding to grow.

The thing that is most wrong with adults is that they have forgotten how to be kids. As adults, we have lost our sense of natural creativity and genuine play. When was the last time that you shuffled your feet through dried, crinkling leaves in the fall? Or the last time that you sat back in the grass and tried to figure out if that puffy, white cloud was shaped like a dog? Nurturing that creative side in us can aid us in finding creative ways to deal with stress and solve problems. Adult play can help our brains stay sharp and resilient.

Schedule time to play and have fun. Buy crossword puzzles and word searches to improve brain function. Get a coloring book to stimulate the mind and boost creativity. There are Mandala coloring books available if you want an "adult" coloring book, which has beautiful shapes and designs. (Just be careful if you look up "adult coloring" at work or you might get fired.) Fill your own toy box with puzzles, games, Play-Doh, and Legos. Who says that stuff is just for kids? Join a team. When was the last time you played dodgeball? Take a class. Pole dancing, anyone? Try an escape room, laser tag, or paintball. There is no better feeling than shooting a zombie with a machine gun in a laser tag event. When you share laughter and fun, you improve your connection to others, as well as, improve your social skills and cooperation with others. When you play, you find an increase in your levels of love, joy, and happiness.

As important as socialization is, we also need to recognize when we need some alone time. It is important to take time out to reflect, reevaluate, regroup, and recharge. If you are an introvert, you know how draining overstimulation can be. Like the bear in the winter goes into hibernation mode, we humans, too, need to hibernate from time to time.

Color Therapy and Psychology

Have you ever wondered why you felt drawn to a particular color? Why did you wear a green shirt today? Why do you feel relaxed in one friend's room and energized in another? We are influenced by color. Color can affect our moods and emotions. Research has found that in general, we associate certain colors with certain emotions.

- Red: aggressiveness, passion, intensity, energy, confidence, stimulating
- Orange: energy, ambition, creativity, enthusiasm, courage, happiness, success
- Yellow: happiness, optimism, cheerful, warmth, confidence, wakefulness
- Green: renewal, peace, prosperity, tranquility, soothing, calming, healing, nature
- Blue: serenity, focus, peace, relaxing, harmony, stability, trust, confidence
- Violet/Purple: Intuition, creativity, spiritual, wisdom, mystery, wealth, power, luxury
- White: purity, cleanliness, innocence, spacious

Color psychology is based on the mental and emotional effects that colors can influence on sighted people. Art therapy often uses color to associate with a person's emotions. Now, that being said, how color affects someone is dependent on one's personal experiences, so it is difficult to make a color universally translated to specific feelings. Personal experiences, culture, background, and preferences play a role in what colors you may be more drawn to.

Even marketing has caught on to the power of color. Ninety percent of impulse buying decisions on products are based solely on color. Red, orange, and yellow tend to whet one's appetite, so it is no accident that McDonald's color scheme is red and yellow. Blue tends to curb appetite, so if you are trying to lose weight, get blue plates. Products and companies like Lowe's, Dell, AT&T, and Wal-mart use the color blue, which signifies trust, dependability, and strength. Whole Foods, Tropicana, and Publix use green as their primary color to represent peacefulness, growth, and health. For a sense of excitement, youthfulness, and boldness, companies like Nintendo, Coca-Cola, Lego, and Target make use of the color red. Hooters wants to create an atmosphere that is friendly and cheerful, so it is no coincidence that they use a lot of orange. Companies and organizations don't pick these color schemes on a whim. There is a lot of science and research that goes into these selections to attract their potential customers.

If you are stressed, green and blue are two great colors to have around. Both have a relaxing and calming effect. Paint a wall one of these colors. According to a Travelodge survey, those who have blue bedrooms sleep an average of seven hours and fifty-two minutes each night. Those whose bedrooms were red had the worst sleep. So if you have trouble sleeping, paint the walls blue or throw on a blue comforter. Invest in some blue or green pillows. Add some green plants into your home. Plants will add oxygen into your environment, and the color is soothing.

You may be thinking this is crazy talk, but there is some science to back it up. Color therapy, also known as chromotherapy or light therapy, uses colored lights to create subtle changes in mood, and it has been practiced for centuries. Light not only enters through your eyes, but it is also absorbed through your skin. For instance, WebMD reported that LED green-light therapy has helped people suffering from migraines. This study worked so well that the trial participants refused to return the lights back to the researchers after the study. As I mentioned in the forest bathing section, people are affected by SAD due to a lack of exposure to light, specifically during the winter months. People, like plants, need to be exposed to different kinds of light. There are actually lights on the market that emit light that replicates the sun. It is quite helpful for people suffering from SAD.

Music

"One good thing about music, when it hits you, you feel no pain."
~ Bob Marley

Music plays a special role in most of our lives. It evokes a response that is universal. It can take you back to a place and time long ago. It can change your mood. It can inspire, or it can make you cry. It can get you through a long morning commute or accompany you in a workout at the gym. Music can help you pass the time while you are doing mundane chores like laundry. Employees have been found to be more productive when allowed to listen to their preferred music choices over those who have no control over their musical choices. But even background music increases performance and accuracy in employees and also enables efficiency in repetitive tasks. Music has been a teacher to us as children, helping us learn the alphabet and numbers. Like with color, advertisers exploit music to get us excited to buy the products that they are peddling. Example: McDonald's jingle for a Big Mac: *"Two all beef patties, special sauce, lettuce, cheese, pickles, onions on a sesame seed bun."* Don't tell me you didn't have that tune playing in your head as you read that line!

It may create a timestamp in your mind. For instance, the song "Amazing" by Aerosmith was popular when I found out that I was pregnant. When my grandfather died, I listened to the song "Creep" by Radiohead as we were driving to the gravesite. Two very different songs, but when I hear them, I am brought back to specific places and times along with all the emotion that went with them. Even listening to "sad" music is beneficial in a cathartic way.

Music has been influencing the human race since nearly the dawn of man. Bone flutes have been dated back to between 40,000-80,000 years ago. The first instrument, however, was the human voice. It is thought that primitive man probably communicated emotion before the constructs of language were established. Before there was writing, our ancestors used music to help them remember things.

The brain's relationship with music is fantastic. When a musician sits down at a piano, several things happen. The brain executes a motor-action plan, which is a sequence of events that unfold in a particular order. Your brain relays information to your fingers as to what pattern of notes to play in what order. As you rehearse these movements repeatedly, you strengthen the neural circuits in your brain. Like the saying, practice makes perfect! Music is also associated with the brain's reward system. As we play or listen to music, dopamine is released. This process is similar to what happens in your brain in response to sex or food, except unlike the other two, there is no survival value involved in music. Oxytocin is also released by singing. It is often referred to as the "cuddle hormone". Serotonin levels can increase after listening to music.

It is proven that music improves the health and function of our brains. By listening to and playing music, we become more intelligent and happier regardless of our stage of life. Children who study music and the arts do better in Math and Science. Stanford University of Medicine investigated the power of music on the mind, and they found that when people listen to music, their attention spans can be increased. They learned this by the brain images of people as they listened to music and even in the pauses in between musical movements and pieces. During these pauses, there was still activity in the brain, which led them to believe that the brain anticipates events to come.

Music influences our behavior. It affects the brain as well as other body structures, which can be observable and measurable. Music is the only sensory experience that can activate all areas of the brain simultaneously. This affects a person's cognitive, emotional, and physical functions. Because of this, music therapy is used successfully in rehabilitation, education, and wellness programs. Vanderbilt Children's Hospital offers a music therapy program to work with children of all ages and their families to create individualized interventions to aid their patients. Music therapy can help with pain management, anxiety, stress, socialization, coping, sensory stimulation, memory building, and enhancing mood. For example, classical music tends to have a calming and relaxing effect. That being said, no matter what type of music, your brain prefers the same kind of music that you do. It depends on personal experiences, background, and preferences, much like with color.

How does this happen? There have been studies that used brain imaging to show that the right hemisphere is activated when listening to music in relation to the emotional experience. Even just imagining music activates this part of the brain. Plato thought that music would arouse different emotions, and there seems to have been a link between music and emotion for most of human existence. Even the tempo of the music affects our moods, for example, slower music seems less joyous than faster rhythms.

A study by Michael H. Thaut, PhD., a Music Professor of Neuroscience, has shown that music's relationship to the brain can actively facilitate the recovery of movement in patients with cerebral palsy, stroke, Parkinson's disease, and traumatic brain injury. Another study called Music Therapy for Depression by A. Maratos, C. Gold, X. Wang, and M. Crawford of patients with memory disorders such as Alzheimer's disease suggested that musical traces can be deeply ingrained and are more resilient to these neurodegenerative influences. Another study from the University of Central Florida found that Parkinson's and Alzheimer's patients responded positively to music. Some studies suggest that learning new skills, like how to play a musical instrument, may possibly help stave off dementia. There is evidence to support that music can decrease the frequency of seizures in children with epilepsy in both awake and sleep states. And yet another study in the Trends in Cognitive Sciences journal showed that patients who listened to music prior to surgery had lower cortisol levels and less anxiety than those who took anti-anxiety medications.

7 MAKING YOUR LIFE EASIER

"Once you replace negative thoughts with positive ones, you'll start having positive results." ~ *Willie Nelson*

Get Organized
Life can be hard. Things don't always go the way that we plan. There is no need for us to make life harder on ourselves than we need to. We tend to make roadblocks for ourselves. We definitely can be our own worst enemy. We procrastinate, which means we put off our happiness. "I'll do it tomorrow." Will you? I'm sure that you say that to yourself all the time. I certainly say it to myself. If tomorrow does ever come, I am sure going to be very busy! Take some of that load off yourself by doing the task NOW!

You can start to make your life easier by getting organized. Before you start to freak out, remember the movie that we talked about earlier, *What About Bob*? Baby steps! You didn't get overweight in one day, and you didn't get disorganized in one day. Take your time. For a significant change, start small and build upon that. Don't overwhelm yourself with a huge task. Start by establishing small routines and then build up from there.

Begin by taking twenty minutes to clean out your sink. You know...the sink that is piled full of dishes right now. That might include taking all of the clean dishes out of the dishwasher, putting them away, and then loading the dirty dishes. Add some soap, hit 'START', and you're off to the races! Next, grab your Ajax and clean the actual sink. Boom! Twenty minutes, and it's done! The sitcom that you were watching isn't even over yet. Nothing is more depressing than waking up and knowing that your kitchen is a mess. Now, you'll wake up to a sense of freedom. The catch is: keep it that way. If your sink is clean today, you may not have to worry about it tomorrow. That frees tomorrow up to focus on the next task. And then the day after tomorrow, the next. See where I'm going with this?

Start by committing to a morning and evening routine. Before you go to bed, take those twenty minutes or less to make sure the sink is clear of dirty dishes or that the clean ones in the dishwasher are put away. Then, pick out the clothes that you want to wear the following day. I know that we all have spent a lot of time trying to decide on what outfit we want to wear. That can make us late for work and put added stress on our morning. By deciding on our wardrobe the night before, we are freeing up some time for our mornings. And I'm sure none of you hit your snooze button multiple times in the morning, do you? I thought so. So I am certain a few extra minutes in the morning would be quite welcomed.

In *What About Bob,* Bob didn't just walk out of his house and jump on a bus to Lake Winnipesaukee. He had to baby step out of the apartment, baby step down the street, baby step to the bus station, and baby step onto the bus. It was a challenging ordeal, to say the least. And it was quite time-consuming as his hesitation kept him from going forward with his goal. But he broke up his main goal into small, attainable goals. By focusing on one step at a time, he was successful. He slowed down and stayed in the moment of the task that he was performing instead of being overwhelmed by the overall project.

The same goes for any overhaul in your life. If you want to lose weight, you could just dump all of the junk food out of your cabinet, and you might successfully lose weight. But will this plan be sustainable in the long run? You may find more success by cutting out sodas for a couple of weeks, and then move on to eliminating cookies or chips. In this manner, your tastes will subtly change, and you will effectively wean yourself from items that may be detrimental to your success, because you will not have the same desire for them. Likewise, if you go full force in the gym on the first day, you may get burned out. And keep in mind your expectations. Again, it took a while to gain the weight, so it will take some time to lose it. Don't get frustrated if you can't fit into that size 2 in the first month of a new exercise plan. The point is to feel better. And if you feel better, you will start to look better, because people will see the happiness that is shining from you.

Get Rid of Clutter

We as Americans love our stuff. We rush to stores on Black Friday to buy stuff for other people. We are on the computer on Cyber Monday to buy even more stuff and have it shipped to us. Companies like Amazon exist to allow us to buy stuff 24-hours a day from the comfort of our pajamas and couch. Legendary comedian George Carlin spoke about how we have so much stuff that we have to buy stuff to put our stuff in. We even rent places to store all of the stuff that we can't fit in the place that we live. We, in fact, have way too much stuff!

Minimalism has become a hot topic. There are tons of books on the market and Youtube.com is loaded with videos on this topic. I watched one of these videos, and it really resonated with me.

Because we live in a capitalist environment, it is no surprise that we are a materialistic, consumer-driven society. But how much of the stuff that we have do we really need? As an experiment, a young lady boxed up all of her excess stuff and put it into storage for one week. She left herself with very little more than her computer, a notebook and pen, clothing for one week, and yoga mat. She limited herself to basic hygiene products to clear the space off on her bathroom counter.

The first step in minimalism is de-cluttering. After work, instead of walking into the barren room and feeling empty, she actually felt refreshed. One gentleman in the video said that if he hadn't used an item in ninety days and didn't plan on using the item in ninety more days, he would eliminate it. At the end of the video, she decided that she did want to have more clothes than just the week allotment, but she would end up donating quite a bit. She enjoyed the open space that minimalism provides, and she noticed that she had more free time to spend outside of the home. How much in your closet do you not wear? Do you really need more than five or six pairs of shoes? How many items of clothing have you not worn in a one year period? Do you own your things or do they own you?

Living Simply

It's not wrong to want nice things, but owning nice things can carry their own levels of stress. You just bought your first new car, but you are afraid someone will ding your door if you park too close to the store. Will someone break into it? Will you get carjacked? Now you have a high monthly car payment and full coverage insurance. You bought yourself a fancy diamond ring, but you are afraid to wear it in case you lose it. Or what if someone sees it and wants to rob you? You fear to leave it home, because what if someone breaks into your house and steals it. You buy a big house, but that big house comes with a big monthly mortgage. If you live simply, you don't have to worry as much about someone stealing your things. You aren't as worried if your things get damaged or lost. In the end, they are just THINGS.

Holding on to things can be unhealthy as well. We can become very attached to our stuff. We really have trouble letting go, figuratively and literally. What is the reason that we can't let go? If we keep these clothes, will people like us? If we get rid of them, will we be lacking in some way? Hoarding is a very real issue, and in a lot of cases, it stems from some sort of fear that we cannot overcome. One way to let go is to think of the people that these items could better service if we were to donate them. In a way, we are being selfish by holding on to them without using them ourselves. Maybe there is a single mother who just got out of an abusive relationship. And maybe this suit or dress that you have shoved in the back of your closet may be the outfit that she can wear to an interview to start her new career. You are withholding an opportunity for someone else because you cannot let go.

"There's a victory in letting go of your expectations." ~ Mike White

8 THE PLAN

"If you don't like the road you're walking, start paving another one." ~ Dolly Parton

What do you value?
A lot of people believe that if they have success, they will find happiness, but in reality, the opposite happens. They are trying to put the cart before the horse. In order to have true success, you have to be happy. Some seek pleasure, wealth, or honor, but they are not the ultimate purpose for life. Aristotle claimed that most would agree that happiness is the ultimate purpose of human existence. Those sentiments are no less true some 2,300 years later. In *Nicomachean Ethics*, he wrote, "He is happy who lives in accordance with complete virtue and is sufficiently equipped with external goods, not for some chance period but throughout a complete life." These virtues would include not only wealth, but also health, knowledge, and relationships.

In order to find your happiness, you have to assess what your values are. What is really important to you? There are hundreds and hundreds of values. What are your key values? Here is an example of some common values:

- Achievement
- Adventure
- Art
- Autonomy
- Awareness
- Balance
- Belonging
- Cleanliness
- Community
- Compassion
- Creativity
- Determination
- Empathy
- Fairness
- Friendships
- Fun
- Gratitude
- Growth
- Happiness
- Honesty
- Humor
- Independence
- Joy
- Kindness
- Knowledge
- Love
- Loyalty
- Meaningfulness
- Openness
- Optimism
- Passion
- Patience
- Peace
- Persistence
- Recognition
- Respect
- Responsibility
- Security
- Solitude
- Spirituality
- Stability
- Success

Setting Intentions

If you have read anything about Yoga, Meditation, or even goal setting, you have probably been told to "set your intention", but what does that mean? According to the dictionary, intention has a few meanings: 1.) an act or instance of determining mentally upon some action or result; 2.) the end or object intended; purpose; 3.) purpose or attitude toward the effect of one's actions or conduct. Goal setting helps us to envision the future and create a plan to reach that future. Intentions allow you to focus on what your values are and invest yourself emotionally.

Setting daily intentions can guide you to achieving happiness. It makes you focus on being in the moment. What do you want from this meeting, encounter, or debate? Your day will be given purpose, and you will have the motivation to reach that purpose. Intentions can make you become more productive, because you will be putting more thought into your actions. You will not think about your limitations, but your potential. You will focus your attention on positive thoughts. Setting intentions can also allow you to observe things that you might have otherwise missed. For instance, if you are working outside today, you might set your intention to notice all of the natural beauty that surrounds you. Instead of getting lost in what you are doing, set the intention to be aware of your surroundings and show gratitude for them.

Unlike setting goals, intentions focus on the moment. It is not something to which you would attach an expectation. When setting intentions, you must ask yourself a few questions: who do you want to be, what do you want to contribute to the world, or how do you want to touch other people's lives? One example of a specific intention would be: "I want to open my heart and my mind to be receptive to any information that will lead me to achieve my goals." How you phrase your intention is just as important as the intention itself. The wording gives it power. For instance, instead of saying, "I hope that this is a good day today", you should alter it to say "I intend to have a good day today." Do you see the difference in the power of the wording? The second version has more confidence and assertiveness.

Intentions let you really think about what is important to you. They come from the heart, therefore, they help you align your heart with your mind. It is a matter of deciding what you want to build, create, be grateful for, or even let go of, like the fears that you want to release. When setting intentions, they should be positive in nature. They should focus on the short term, because they might change. If you think it, you become it. Intentions are endless. Here are some examples:
1. Find balance
2. Open the mind and heart
3. Peace
4. Embrace change
5. Love and to love unconditionally
6. Connect with others
7. To manifest happiness
8. To lead by example
9. Make someone smile each day

Goal Setting

Most of us have taken a road trip at some time. Maybe we drove to Florida for vacation or maybe we wanted to visit a new city. We didn't just jump in the car and go. We needed to make a plan. To get there directly and in a timely manner, we probably used GPS or a map. We didn't just blindly head off in a direction. We had to know where we were going. Goal setting is that map that gets us to our destination.

First, you must decide what it is that you want to do. Second, you must determine why. You have to ask yourself: "Do I want to be ____ because ____ or ____?"

For example: "Do I want to be a comedian because of passion or money?" Doing anything just for the money may not be a strong enough motivator. You may not find yourself as invested in making the goal a reality. "Do I want to have a family because of my family's expectations or because it is fulfilling?" Is this goal something that you really want for yourself? If you are doing something for anyone other than yourself, you may not find happiness and may end up feeling resentful. No one can want this goal more than you do. You have to be your own champion.

Once you realize what you want to do, you have to come up with a plan to achieve it. Much like when you go on a trip, you have to map out the route that you want to take. Goal setting allows you to think about what you want to do and what are the steps that you need to take to reach that destination.

One method of goal setting is to set SMART goals.
- **Specific**
- **Measurable**
- **Attainable**
- **Realistic**
- **Timely**

Specific. Your goal should be as specific as possible to be able to make a detailed plan of action. This is the: who, what, when, where, and why. Saying "I want to be an author" isn't very specific. Instead, you may want to say "I want to be an author with a self-published book on stress management. I want to combine this with speaking engagements." This is a bit more specific and gives you some direction on how to pursue your goal.

In the Specific category, I mentioned that you must ask yourself certain questions: who, what, when, where, and why. Who is involved? What do you want to accomplish? Where will you accomplish it and when? Which requirements need to be met? I think that the most important question is WHY. Why are you doing this? Do you know what your reasons are for setting this goal? What is the purpose of the goal? What are the benefits? When people are asked why they are setting that specific goal, they may give a variety of answers. Maybe they want to make more money. Maybe they are searching for autonomy. They may be seeking recognition. Maybe this is something they are passionate about. The reason why is very telling on how committed you are to reaching your goal. If it is just for money, how invested are you really? If it is because you are so passionate about it that you can't imagine doing anything else, you are going to be much more invested in accomplishing your goal. "I want to be an author with a self-published book on stress management, because I have an important message to put out into the world that can help a lot of people with the same issues that I have." That is a much stronger *why* than "I want to be an author to make a lot of money."

Measurable. Can you measure your progress or success with pursuing your goal? How will you hold yourself accountable? This allows you to track your progress. A good way to do this is to set smaller goals that work toward your main goal. "I want to complete my manuscript in the next three months." You have given yourself a time table for the first leg of your journey. You will know if you have accomplished this if your manuscript is finished in the allotted time.

It is also important to be thoughtful in how you articulate your goal as well as your intention. It is not enough to say, "I want to *try* to finish my manuscript in three months." You must be more definitive and concrete in your goal. As Yoda says in *The Empire*

Strikes Back, "Try not. Do...or do not. There is no try." If you say you are going to try to do something, you might as well just say that you aren't going to do it. How many times have you said that you would try to do something and then didn't? To make a measurable goal, you should rephrase this goal to say, "I will finish my manuscript in three months."

Attainable. Is this a goal that can be attained? You want goals that push you, but not that are beyond your reach. Do you have the abilities and skills to achieve this goal? Are you financially capable to reach it? What is your attitude toward the goal? Can it be done?

Realistic. Is the goal realistic as well as the timeframe? "I want to be on Oprah's Book Club in six months." Well, unless you have some connections, word of mouth spreads, or you are very lucky, this goal may not come to light. Your goal should be challenging or you won't take it seriously. If it is too challenging, it can overwhelm you.

Timely. This is your timeframe. It should help to keep you motivated and accountable. For this, you may state "I want to be a self-published author with my book on stress management being published in six months." Now, you have given yourself a time table. You will know if you are on the right path if you can reach this goal within the allotted timeframe. A timeframe is very important, because it creates a sense of urgency. Without a timeframe, you could allow yourself to keep putting off tasks involved in achieving your goal. It also creates a focal point for you.

Remember when you were in first grade, and your teacher gave you a gold star for completing your work or doing a chore? Remember how great you felt!? You probably felt proud and very motivated to do more good so that you could get more stars. A great way to make sure you reach these goals is to give yourself small rewards after each small goal is achieved. Now, if your goal is to lose weight or start an exercise program, you may not want to reward yourself with a cheesecake. Maybe instead, a more reasonable reward would be to get a massage or to go see a movie. Pick a reward that doesn't distract you or conflict with your goal. Rewards are a great way to stay on the path and stay focused.

Remember the movie *What About Bob*? In the movie, Bob was crippled with anxiety and panic. He could scarcely leave the house. In order to reach his goal of going to the doctor to seek help, he created small goals for himself. In Dr. Leo Marvin's fictitious book "Baby Steps", the doctor addresses the topic of taking smaller, manageable steps to reach your goal. If your goal is to go to the doctor, as Bob had done, instead of worrying about the end result, the doctor guided him to first focus on walking out the apartment door, then walking out of the building door, then getting on a bus, and so on.

Bob got very overwhelmed at the notion of all that was involved in reaching his goal of getting to the doctor's office. It created much panic and stress in his mind and body. So instead, he focused on walking out of the office door. Success! That motivated him to walk back in. Another success! Baby steps around the office... success! This illustrated to him that he was capable of reaching his goal. This also creates a snowball effect. The more action that you take, the more success you can achieve. When one small goal is reached, you are motivated to take on another small goal without the stress of becoming overwhelmed. You feel good about your accomplishment and it creates a drive in you to want to do more. Give yourself a pat on the back and a little hurray.

Conversely, do not beat yourself up if you do not achieve your goal or if you procrastinate. The more negatively that you reinforce your actions, the fewer actions you will want to take. Like with intentions, you must keep your goals positive. Encourage yourself with positive self-talk. Keep giving yourself gold stars for the work that you accomplish. Pat yourself on the back even if no one else does.

Nashville is a tourist town. There are tons of bars with music cascading out of them from the moment the doors open until the bars close. I had the idea of starting a bar crawl. No one else was doing one at the time. I felt that I was qualified, because I knew a lot of the downtown history already. I knew what bars I felt would be good for people to visit that they may not have known about. I felt that with my background as a stand-up comedian that I could be an entertaining guide. I felt that I had developed a product that was very different than anything else that was currently being offered. I found my niche. I was very excited and anxious about the idea of starting my own business, but I just knew that this could be successful. There were already several tours on the market, but nothing like what I wanted to offer.

I approached my friend about my idea, and she quickly shot me down. "No one is going to pay you to take them to bars." The words stabbed me in the heart. Maybe she was right. Maybe that was an outrageous idea, after all, would I have paid for something like that? But I did not listen to her, and I went forward with my marketing plan. Seven years later, and I am still successful. Even now, she admits how wrong she was. If I had listened to her criticism and pessimism, I would not have started my own business and would not have made my living for seven years doing what I love.

Listening to criticism is fine. It may force you to look at different angles that you had not thought of. BUT letting criticism stop you is not fine. Use criticism as a learning tool, not a stopping point. Take into consideration those cautious points, but if you still feel like you have a worthy product, don't let a Negative Nancy hold you back. Also, don't let your own negative self-talk prevent you from taking the first steps toward your goal or dream. No risk, no reward.

Some people spend too much time in the goal setting phase. Do not spend so much time in the goal-setting or the planning phase that you avoid or get distracted from taking action. Some people say that they must wait for the right or perfect time. There is no such thing as perfect. There is no perfect person, no perfect time, or no perfect situation. If you wait for perfect, chances are that it will never come.

What is your passion?
You will be more successful in reaching your goal if it is something that you are passionate about and that you really enjoy doing. If your goal is to be an author, but you hate writing, is that really an appropriate goal for you? How many of us are doing things because we feel that we are *supposed* to do them and not because we *want* to do them? Are these expectations our own or someone else's? When I was young, it was typical, if not expected, that you graduate high school, get married, and have children. That is what everyone did. But I did not feel like that was my path. Instead, I decided to go to college. That was unheard of in my family at the time. I was the first one to graduate college. Did I have kids? Yes. Did I get married? No. I did not feel that marriage was a priority to me. When thinking about your passion, you have to take into consideration what is a priority to you.

Katharine Hepburn began acting while studying at Bryn Mawr College. She had decided that acting was her passion. Because of this, she made the conscious choice to not have children. She felt that if she wanted to seriously pursue acting as a profession that she would not be able to adequately give the attention to children that they would need. She realized that to be a professional actor to the caliber that she desired that she would have to make acting a priority over having a family. She was married in her twenties, but was not fully committed to the marriage as she was to acting, so they divorced. She knew who she was as a person. She had said after she divorced that "I liked the idea of being my own single self". She made the decision to never remarry.

When you realize your passion and want to pursue it, you sometimes may have to make some sacrifices in your life. Maybe you have to put off buying a house or having children. Maybe you have to cut back on finances to afford your dream. You have to ask yourself how badly do you really want this thing, and where does it fall on your list of priorities? Nothing ventured, nothing gained.

In finding your passion, another exercise that you can consider is to ask yourself "what would you like to do if money wasn't an obstacle or a factor?" This will call for some serious reflection and contemplation. If you did not have to worry about bills or mortgages, what would you like to pursue? Our need for financial stability is important for our physical and mental well-being, but it can also create a barrier to keep us from reaching our goals. If it is possible to put these fears to the side for a moment, we can get an idea of what we really want.

That is not to say that you should quit your job, stop paying your bills, and let your house go into foreclosure, but this exercise should act as a motivator to really get you thinking about what it is that you want to do with your life. It can also give you a glimpse of a potential plan outline. If you can visualize what you want to do, that is the first step toward making it a reality. Maybe you can put your plan into action on the weekends or work at it on your lunch breaks. You can make it happen if you want it badly enough and are passionate about it. You have to find the time.

Visualization Into Realization

Look around your home or office. Everything you see there was once in someone else's imagination. Before you create anything, you first imagine it. That table was once a doodle on someone's notepad. Your television was someone else's daydream. Every book on your bookshelf or every movie in your collection started out as someone's idea. It all starts with a thought.

If you say it, you become it. Also, if you see it, you can be it. This may sound cliché, but it is very true. You may not be aware of how powerful visualization can be, but you probably do it every day. If you are bowling, before you roll the ball, do you ever envision the pins all falling down? If you are baking a cake, do you imagine how the finished product will look? If so, you were using visualization. Visualization is basically a mental rehearsal or practice. Conversely, have you ever worried about a problem and anticipated it ending badly? Do you picture the worst? That is also visualization, but in this case, you are focusing on what you do not want. You may have worried so much about something that it actually happened. You just created something that you did not want. It became a self-fulfilling prophecy.

With visualization, you want to anticipate a positive outcome. You are seeing your goal as if it is already completed. If you want a new house, see yourself sitting on the front porch swing. If you are up for a promotion, you want to use imagery that has you already in the position for which are vying. See yourself in your new office sitting behind your new desk with your new nameplate sitting on it. You want to see yourself already doing it, already a success! If you want to be a photographer, visualize yourself on the savannah photographing majestic lions. If your dream is to be a singer, picture yourself on a stage in front of thousands of adoring fans. And if you are dreaming, why not dream big!

Research has shown that people improve their performance when they imagine themselves performing a task beforehand. The most successful people use visualization to make their dreams into realities. Athletes, the rich, and the super successful all use this skill. It is a skill just like any other and takes practice to make it work effectively. It is a great tool to help program your brain, specifically your subconscious. It activates neural pathways and stimulates the sympathetic nervous system. Our heart rate, breathing, and blood pressure increase, much like in a fight-flight-freeze response. It tricks our bodies into thinking that we are physically executing the same actions that we are envisioning. When you repeatedly imagine yourself performing a task, it conditions your neural pathways. It does this in such a way that when you go to actually perform it, the action feels familiar. This enhances your motivation as well as your confidence.

Visualization, also known as mental imagery, can help you to manifest the life that you want. First, you need to know what it is that you want. To do this, we must understand what we value.

Next, you want to create a very clear vision of what you want. Some people may do this by writing it down in a journal or on index cards or creating a vision board. Post the cards on your refrigerator, on your bathroom mirror, or next to your bed. A vision board, or dream board, is a collage of images and affirmations of your dreams. It serves the purpose of inspiring and motivating you. This is a popular technique used in the law of attraction. It helps you concentrate and maintain focus on your goals. When Jack Canfield was writing *Chicken Soup for the Soul*, he made a mock-up copy of the New York Times bestseller list with *Chicken Soup for the Soul* in the number one spot in his desired category. He placed these prints all over his office, and in less than two years, the book was number one in that category, staying there for over a year!

Affirmations are a great tool, too. Repeatedly saying something cements it into your psyche. When you say something often enough, your brain believes it to be the truth. It cannot distinguish the difference. The same goes for visualizations, especially if your visions and affirmations are in the present tense. Instead of saying "I want to be an artist," say "I am a successful, talented artist." You are putting it in the current tense. If you run your visualization exercises often enough in your mind, your mind is incapable of determining whether it has really happened or not. As far as your brain is concerned, it happened. This is the concept of neuroplasticity.

Next, bring your senses into the visualization. Imagine the sights, sounds, smells, and even tastes of what it will be like to be in the life that you want. If you want a brand new car, smell that new car scent. Feel the leather seats and steering wheel. See yourself in the driver's seat. As for taste, don't lick anything. That's gross. The more detailed that you can get, the more effective the visualization will be. This will make an emotional investment in your visualization. Imagine that you are in a movie theater, and your dreams are playing out on the big screen. If you can see it, you can be it!

Take five to ten minutes each day to focus on your visualizations. Done daily, just a few minutes will accomplish so much, but don't spend so much time daydreaming that you don't actually put your goals into action. If you are incorporating meditation into your daily routine, try doing your visualizations after you finish meditating. If you are using affirmations, don't just read them to yourself. Saying them out loud with feeling will have a greater impact.

Now, it's time to take action! You can see what you want, so now take the steps to make it a reality. Just do it. You may start to feel overwhelmed that your dream is too big. How can you take steps to achieve something so great? Don't concern yourself with how far away the end point is. Instead, stay focused on the present moment. What can you do today to get closer to your goal? Don't worry about tomorrow. After all, tomorrow never comes. What can you do now to make yourself better than you were yesterday?

JUST DO IT!

The law of attraction basically means that positive begets positive and negative begets negative. You put out into the world what you want to bring back. This is true in most cultures. For instance, the Golden Rule: do unto others as you would have them do unto you. Other cultures and religions have similar philosophies. Some call it threefold: whatever you put out into the world comes back to you threefold. If you put out negative thoughts and actions, do not be surprised if negativity is all that you experience. Likewise, if you put out positivity, you will notice increased positivity in your life. Will you still hit some road bumps and potholes? Of course, but the more positively you live, the better equipped you will be to deal with these annoyances. In fact, when you do hit these potholes, visualize yourself overcoming them.

Create a vision board. A vision board is a tool that you can use to put your goals into focus. They allow you to clarify what you want by giving it a tangible image that you can concentrate on. You can use a cork board or just copy images to a piece of paper or poster board to make your collage. I make my vision boards in a Word document on my computer with clips of various pictures and words.

Take it a step further. Imagine your goal as if it has already happened. Carry yourself as you would if you had already achieved what you desired. Hold your head up and walk with confidence. Imagine that your business is already off the ground and successful. Envision your new house totally furnished as you sit on the couch with the fireplace roaring. See yourself in the new body after you have put in so much work with diet and exercise. Really feel good about these changes as if they already exist.

A Personal Mission Statement
When you start a business, one of the first things that you do is to create a mission statement. It identifies what your organization does and gives the organization structure. It is the Who, What, When, Where, Why, and How of your organization. A personal mission statement is similar in that it identifies your core values and beliefs. It articulates what you are all about. It paints a picture of what success looks like to you.

When writing your own personal mission statement, you will reflect on your past successes. What worked for you? Identify your personal values and goals. Your personal mission statement will allow you to dream, but also keep you grounded in reality. It is not set in stone; your personal mission statement may change over time. Like you, your mission statement may evolve. It will create boundaries for you to work within. You will evaluate all the aspects of your life as it pertains to your goal, and thus, your mission statement. It will help you maintain focus and avoid distractions. This will also come in handy with future decision making.

To write your own personal mission statement, you must answer

these questions:
- **WHO?** Who is your best you? Who are you creating this goal for? Who is your customer or audience?
- **WHAT?** What is important to you? What do you want to do? What do you want to leave as your legacy? What are your skills, values, passions, or dreams?
- **WHEN?** Do you have a timeframe you are working within? Where do you see yourself in one, five, or ten years?
- **WHERE?** Where will this take place? Where do you want to go?
- **WHY?** What is the purpose of your plan? Why do you want to do this?

It does not have to be long. Just a line or two should sum up what you are in a clear and concise manner. An example would be: *"To inspire change and to positively impact the lives of everyone that I meet."*

Oprah Winfrey's personal mission statement looks like this: *"To be a teacher. And to be known for inspiring my students to be more than they thought they could be."*

9 TAKING ACTION

"Remember, tomorrow is promised to no one." ~ Walter Payton

ACTION Steps
Now, you go from talking the talk to walking the walk. All the planning in the world does not matter until you put it into action.

Whether you want to achieve your goals or to make a sale, take these ACTION steps:
- **A**ctively Approach your goal
- **C**oncentrate (avoid distractions)
- **T**hinking backwards and flip your Thinking
- **I**magine yourself with goal completed
- **O**btainable goals and an Optimistic Outlook
- **N**eeds to be met

To achieve your goals, you have to take an **active** approach. Get off the couch. Stay off of Facebook. Activity begets more activity. Once you complete a few small goals, the more goals that you will want to accomplish, but it is a matter of starting to take the first step. All the planning in the world does not matter if you don't take action.

Action:
- If you want to be a writer, sit in front of a keyboard.
- If you want to be a painter, sit in front of an easel.
- If you want to be an entrepreneur, start a business.

Concentrate on your goals. You must keep focus by staying in the moment. Don't let yourself get distracted by the television or Youtube. Put down the video controller. If it does not pertain to your goal, it does not need your focus. Anything else is considered a distraction and will keep you from your potential.

Another C is **Competition**. Don't compare yourself to others. We may spend time looking at what our peers are doing and wondering why we are not at the same level of success of development that they are. *"Why don't I have a nice house like Bob? Why don't I have a fancy car like Lois?"* Your only competition is with yourself. Instead of concerning yourself with someone else's progress, focus only on your own. Are you better today than you were yesterday? Are you living up to your potential?

Look at a time when you were successful. When did you try to outdo yourself? Even if it seems insignificant right now, even a small victory is proof of your accomplishments. When I was a teenager, I worked at the mall at a men's clothing store called Chess King. I became top salesman consistently. I wasn't concerned with beating the other salespeople as much as I wanted to beat my own sales numbers from the previous week or month. I tried to compete with myself instead of competing with others.

If negativity has been getting in your way, you must flip your **thinking**. Instead of focusing on what you do not want in your life, turn your thoughts to what you do want. For example, instead of saying "*I don't want to be poor*", replace it with "*I want to be financially secure and have a great amount of disposable income.*" Dismiss any negative thoughts that creep into your mind and replace them with positive ones. Instead of "*I'm so lazy*", exchange it for "*I am relaxed and my adaptable.*"

Another way to flip your thinking is to **think backwards**. If you know what your destination is, take the steps backwards to see how you get there. For instance, if your goal is to be on Saturday Night Live, you will want to look at other people that have gotten to that point and see what steps they took to get there. They all have agents. Maybe before SNL, they were in improvisational comedy, which most were. From there, you would research with improv schools they came from. Then you will realize that before they began performing improv, they had taken classes at that improv school. A diagram of this path may look something like this:

Improv School to Become a Cast Member of School to Get an Agent to SNL

This is quite simplistic, but you get the idea of the path that they most likely took to get to their level of success.

Some people may become discouraged if the path that they envision takes a detour. It may be discouraging when it is not a straight path. Instead of getting from A to B, we may end up going from A to D to C to B. Instead of getting frustrated, we must step back and enjoy the process. After all, life is a journey, not a destination.

Your **imagination** is a great tool. Visualize yourself doing what you want. Envision that you have already completed your goal and are successful. Use your internal control. Harness your brain's power with meditation. What is success to you? What does it look like?

Set small, **obtainable** goals. Instead of focusing on how far away your goal may seem, taking baby steps to get there.

Another O is **optimism**. You will find happiness and success with a positive outlook. You have to believe that you can achieve your goal. You also have to believe that you are worthy of success.

What do you **need**? What is it that you want to ultimately get from your goal? What do you need to be able to reach your goal?

"The secret of getting ahead is getting started." ~ *Mark Twain*

Why Do We Fail?

Why don't we achieve our goals?
- Procrastination
- Distractions
- Overwhelmed
- Self-Defeating/Negative/Self-Sabotaging
- Hardest Part: Getting Up, Getting Out, Getting Started

What makes us fail? We make lists, schedules, etc., but they don't work. Hours fly by wasted doing anything other than working on our goals.

- On sofa
- In bed
- Internet surfing
- Reading

These distractions are our excuses to delay.

What do we need to do to combat this?
- Small, obtainable goals – avoid becoming overwhelmed – set daily goals
- Accountability
- Flip your thinking (Negative to Positive)
- Find out what you want to do (and why)

We often may get overwhelmed by how enormous the feat may seem. It is easier for us to do nothing than to attempt to climb this mountain. But if we make small, obtainable goals for ourselves, we will avoid being overwhelmed. Instead of looking at the top of the mountain and thinking you'll never make it, focus on taking the first step. As in the old saying, a thousand-mile journey begins with one step. Before you know it, you will be fifteen steps into your journey, and then fifty, and so on. The trick is to not beat yourself up if you go a day with only making one step.

When you begin working out at the gym, it may seem like you have bitten off more than you can chew. Ten minutes on the treadmill may seem like a million years. But soon, you will build up to twenty, and before you know it, you are doing forty-five minutes. Once you get in the habit of hitting the gym, you miss it if you have to skip a session. It becomes part of your routine and part of you, but you had to work up to it to get to that point.

Eric Clapton did not wake up one day, pick up a guitar, and start playing. He practiced...a lot! In interviews, I have heard him speak of practicing for hours and hours every day. He practiced so much that his fingers would actually bleed. But he knew what he wanted. He knew that if he wanted to be the best in his field, it required a strong determination and a great amount of work. But because of his dedication, he is the only three-time inductee into the Rock and Roll Hall of Fame.

You are going to fail sometimes. But that's okay. Those failures can also be looked at as steps to success. Every *"no"* that you hear gets you that much close to a *"yes"*. A baseball player doesn't just pick up a bat and hit a home run. It takes practice. But even the best players face defeat. Reggie Jackson holds the record for most strikeouts with a career 2,597 strikeouts. That is a lot of failures. But he also has a record of 563 home runs. He struck out a lot, but it took those 2,597 failures to create 563 successes.

Failure is not necessarily a bad thing. Our failures can be teaching tools. Thomas Edison once said something to the effect of "I didn't fail one thousand times. I've just found one thousand ways that didn't work." I was unable to find the actual quote, but you get the picture. It is not that we fall; it is that we get back up and do not quit. For example, if one were to drop a rubber ball, it doesn't just stay down; it bounces back. And the harder you drop it, the stronger it bounces back.

One reason that we fail to take action is due to our lack of focus. You may have given yourself a deadline, but it is not concrete. A passive deadline creates no sense of urgency. Then, if we do not stick to our deadlines, we beat ourselves up when our goal is not reached or a deadline not completed. That only makes us feel terrible about ourselves and further makes us avoid taking future actions. We become our own worst enemies.

At times, we may beat ourselves up because we feel "stupid". It is totally fine to feel that way. It is arrogant to think that you know it all. You should constantly be learning. Be aware that you don't know it all. Be open to knowledge. Conversely, it can also be said that you know more than you think you do. Give yourself some credit.

Timing is everything....WRONG! Again, there is no perfect time. We all think "I'll be happy when..." We have all been guilty of that from time to time. "I'll be happy when I get this position." "I'll be happy when I get a new house or a new car." You are putting your happiness on a time table. You are delaying your happiness for a time period that will never exist. Be happy now. You only have now. The past is gone, and the future never comes. You must be in the present. We are not guaranteed tomorrow. Anything could happen. We may face illness, loss, even death, so today should be lived to its fullest. And if you are living in the moment, it is senseless to deny yourself a second of happiness.

The hardest part about reaching your goal is starting. When working on *Annie Hall*, Woody Allen was interviewed and quoted as saying, "Eighty percent of success is showing up."

"Never let the fear of striking out get in your way." ~ Babe Ruth

Accountabili-buddies

To be successful at reaching your goal, you have to be accountable for your actions. Sometimes, if we are left to our own devices, we may sit and binge watch Netflix. It can be difficult for us to make ourselves culpable. A good way to be accountable is to get a buddy who is also trying to accomplish a goal and keep tabs on each other. It can make for some good brainstorming as well as making sure that we are keeping our momentum going.

In an episode of *South Park* called "Cartman Sucks", Butters must attend a gay conversion therapy camp. In this camp, each boy is paired up with an "accountabili-buddy" who is there to keep each other on task and exchange feedback. This buddy system helps to keep you from straying from the path toward your goal. This person keeps you responsible for your actions. Without an "accountabili-buddy", you may make excuses for not taking action, and therefore, you make no progress. Some people are just not good at managing themselves. If left to their own devices, they procrastinate. Without having someone to answer to, we may do nothing. Without one, it is easy for us to slip into our pattern of putting our tasks off until tomorrow. Remember, tomorrow never comes!

Find someone that you trust and respect to be your "accountabili-buddy", but someone who will see through your crap. A good "accountabili-buddy" will not take your excuses as valid reasons for not completing your goals. They do not do the work for you, but make sure you stay on track. It is great if you can find someone who needs an "accountabili-buddy", too.

If you are planning a new exercise program, having an "accountabili-buddy" might make you stick to the plan. You will be more motivated to get out of bed and to the gym if you know that your buddy is there waiting for you. You will make sure you are not late for your yoga class if you know that you want a mat next to your buddy. You might justify letting yourself down, but it is harder for you to let someone else down.

Say No To Multi-tasking

For years, you were told that you had to learn to multi-task. Even in college, I remember a professor saying that the industry would be looking for people that had a number of skills instead of a specialization. Today, we are finding that just is not necessarily the case. In our world of having many irons in the fire, we have become overextended, overworked, and overburdened. We start something new before we have had a chance to finish what we were just working on. And in the end, we have several things we are working on, but nothing is finished. You probably have a dozen windows open on your computer right now, don't you? With so many plates spinning in the air, it is only a matter of time before they come crashing down on us.

Multitasking is a form of distraction. Instead of doing a million things at once, do one thing, focused, at a time. Pick one task and work on it until completion. Pay attention fully to whatever is in front of you. Concentrate on one thing at a time. If you get tired, take several breaks if needed.

Find Mindfulness and Meaning

Be fully present in what you are doing. Show compassion by really listening to others. Put all of your attention into what you are currently doing. Mindfully set your expectation. Love what you do. In the movie *Groundhog Day*, Phil gets up every day to same old, same old. Every day is the same. He finally realizes that if he wants change, he must make the most of his time. He learns to play piano, designs ice sculptures, makes a snowman, forges relationships with the townspeople, and even changes a tire in record time. Instead of becoming stifled by the monotony of having to repeat the same day over and over, he finds ways to make the experience more interesting for himself. Even though each day was essentially the same, he found little ways to make each one different, and in doing so, he found ways to cope with his frustrating circumstances.

Find meaning in jobs that you don't think you love. If you cannot quit your job, you have to find something about it that you love. When I was working at the mall as a teenager, to make my job seem more interesting, I gave myself a title. I thought that the title Sales Associate was too common and ordinary. I wanted to spice it up and make myself feel more engaged at work. I gave myself the title of Wardrobe Consultant. Now, this was not a real title. I was not supposed to put it on my name tag, but I took the labeler gun and added this new designation to my name tag. Did my job change at all? No, but my attitude about it did. I found a new zest and pride for my work and proudly introduced myself with this new moniker. It was the same job, but that little change in attitude made the job feel more important, and it made me feel like more of an expert and gave the job purpose and meaning. I had found a way to make lemonade from lemons.

Finding happiness is important for having satisfaction in life, but so is meaning. Ask yourself why you are there in the first place. At one point, you liked it. Now, you just have to remember why and find that spark again. Maybe you have a family to support. That's great, because it means that you are contributing to the well-being of others. You may not love being there, but this shows that there is a higher purpose in what you are doing. Look back over your list of values and apply them to your current situation. For instance, if you value kindness or thoughtfulness, try bringing a co-worker a cup of coffee when you go get yourself one. This will make you feel better, and it will also unexpectedly brighten up their day.

When you are in a job that you don't enjoy, look at this as an opportunity to look toward the future and imagine no longer being there, but pursuing your goals. Your current situation is what is going to get you to that point. Patience is what is needed until you reach that point. You may not have something else lined up yet, but there will be.

When you are in a job that you do not like, the inclination is to get out. That is not always an option. You still have to pay rent and bills, put food on the table, and put clothes on your back. If you cannot leave, you need to find ways to cope.

What specifically is it that you dislike about your job? Is there too much workload? Do you dislike a co-worker? A boss? Are you underpaid? Have you made steps to correct these issues? Does your boss know your complaints? Most people do not even take the chance to convey their grievances to their employers. Maybe if you brought it to your boss' attention that you have not had a raise in six months, he could fix it. Maybe if she knew you were inundated with your workload, she could delegate some of it to other employees. If the problem is with a co-worker, maybe you could speak to them. If that did not work, maybe the supervisor could intervene. Maybe you could be moved to another department. Do not wallow in self-pity if you have not exhausted all of your possible avenues for correcting the issues.

Maybe it is not an issue of changing the situation, but changing your perspective. Your mind has a lot of power over your circumstances. Are you looking at the glass half empty or half full? When you are feeling negative about a situation, those feelings can snowball out of control if you do not correct them and convert them into positive feelings. Instead of looking at this as just a paycheck, view your job as a way of refining your skills and stepping up to new challenges. You have to put a lid on the stinkin' thinkin'.

Put your best foot forward. Instead of just going through the motions and putting in the bare minimum, do your best work. In the movie *Office Space*, Joanna wore her fifteen pieces of "flair", which was the bare minimum. If she had put in a slight bit more effort and slapped on a few more pieces of flair, her boss would not have been on her back. The same goes for Peter. He came in late, left early, checked out at his desk, and played Tetris. Like Joanna, if he did put in more effort, he felt that he would not see any benefit for himself. Unbeknownst to him, though, when he was open and honest to the Bobs and spoke openly about his grievances, he was rewarded with a promotion and a raise.

A Job, a Career, or a Calling
Why are you doing this work? Is it for money? Is it a career stepping stone? Is it fulfilling your calling?

We fail to know what we really want. We may get frustrated with our current job, but don't know what to do about it. If your job seems to be the problem, ask yourself if this is a job, a career, or a calling. A job does not fulfill our deeper needs. A career is the next level. A calling is where your passion lives. To be able to tell the difference, you must determine what you feel your purpose is. What do you feel the purpose of life is? For some, it is to help others and make other people happy. To others, it is love itself. Whatever you feel your purpose is, it gives your life meaning.

A job is often viewed as a means to an end. It affords us to keep a roof over our heads and food on the table. It provides us the basic necessities of life. Its main purpose is to earn a paycheck, although there may be benefits and other perks available. With a job, one is not necessarily seeking a place to learn, gain experience, or create connections.

A career comes with an air of prestige. There may be levels to work up to, i.e. the corporate ladder. Titles may be involved, as well as levels of power. There may be more opportunities for training and advancement. One may have a more long-term vision for their future.

A calling has more of an alignment with their chosen vocation and their identity. It may involve more of a sense of pride. Besides being financially and emotionally fulfilling, a calling implies that the work has more meaning to the person. It is personal and in line with one's values. They feel a sense of purpose.

What is your calling? What would you do if money wasn't a factor? What if fear wasn't a factor? Most know down deep what that is.

One way of determining your calling is to decide what is your motivation? Dr. Joe Dispenza believes that there are five types of Motivation:
- Purpose
- Personal connection
- Ethics
- Ego-centered
- Money

Money is the lowest form of motivation. Next is the need to satisfy the ego. Purpose is the highest level of motivation for it involves meaning. What level of motivation you feel determines how committed you will be to following through with action. When we live with purpose, we feel more fulfilled.

The ANSWER

Everything is sales. No matter what you do in life, more than likely it will be some form of sales. If you are an artist, you are selling your talent. If you are a singer, you are selling your music and merchandise. If you are a writer, you are selling your works. Everything is sales, and everything is marketing.

When I worked at Chess King, they had a sales plan that they called ANSWER. It was a method that could be used to sell anything, including you. The store chain may have closed, but the plan is still as viable today as it was in the 1980s.

The ANSWER consisted of these principles:
- **A**pproach the Customer
- Determine the Customer's **N**eeds
- **S**how the Merchandise
- **W**elcome and Overcome Objectives
- **E**ncourage the Closing of the Sale

- Suggest **R**elated Items

In most goals that you set, there will be a customer. Who are your readers if you are writing a book? If you are going to be giving a speech, who is your audience? Who is your goal serving? You have to know who you are trying to reach in order to figure out how to approach them. Once you know who they are, you must make your move.

What are your customers looking for? What do they need? If your audience is looking for a way to manage stress, you need to be able to give that to them. If they need a minivan, but all you have in stock are sports cars, you may not make a sale unless you can convince them that a sports car is what they need.

Once you have the customer's attention, you have to show them what you've got. You have to be knowledgeable and make them excited about what you have to offer. If they have reservations about what you are offering, you have to overcome those objections. Most objections fall into the categories of:
- Price - Is what you are offering too expensive for them? If the price is the issue, maybe you need to help them justify the cost.
- Quality - Maybe they are unsure of the quality. This is where knowledge of the product comes into play.
- Trust - They may not trust your relationship. Being forthcoming with information is critical in such a situation. This may be where testimonials would be beneficial.
- Complacency and Fear of Change - Fear keeps us from reaching our potential. You have to show them how change will create a positive outcome for them.
- Timeliness – They may say that they will look for what you are offering later on. You need to show them why they need what you have to offer now.

- Authority - The person that you are speaking with may not be the decision maker. In this case, you need to find out who is the person that is capable of signing off.

To overcome objections, you must listen to their issue, acknowledge their concerns, explore solutions, and then respond properly. You can do that by showing the benefits of using your services.

Once they show interest in your wares, get them to make a commitment. That could be having them buy your service or product. If you are a performing artist or a public speaker, get them to book you. Suggest related items. If you selling shoes, suggest socks. If you are selling your book, offer a private coaching session. This will increase the money you will be making by adding on to your initial sale.

"Failure is unimportant. It takes courage to make a fool of yourself." ~ Charlie Chaplin

10 TIME MANAGEMENT

"The way to get started is to quit talking and begin doing." ~ Walt Disney

Time is the most precious commodity that we have. Unlike money, it is finite in supply and cannot be replenished. Once it is gone, it is gone forever. This is why we must make the most of the time that we have. The great thing about time is that it is unbiased. It does not care what your age, race, sex, income, or religion is. You have the same as anyone else regardless. Whether you are rich or poor, black or white, male or female, your time is the same. It is not about how much time you have, but rather what you do with it.

Are you spending your time wisely or frittering it away? If you found that you only had one year left to live, how would you plan on spending it? Most of us are not given the luxury of knowing how much time we have. Therefore, to effectively utilize it, we may want to spend it as if we only have a short time left to get the most out of it. We want to maximize our productivity. If you are given a month to complete a project, there are many of us that fall into the procrastination trap and put it off until the last minute.

How many of us actually take advantage of the extra time and put it to good use? It is not enough to set your goals, but you have to get serious about avoiding distractions.

Most of us claim that we do not have enough time. We spend one-third of our time in bed. Most of us spend twenty-five percent of our time at work. Somehow, we have to balance the rest of the time that we have getting chores finished, socializing, spending it with our family, and somewhere in there, find a few minutes to set aside and commit to pursuing our goals. Balance is the key. Without balance, we become stressed and lose sight of our happiness. It is crucial to balance all of the aspects of our lives: work, family, friends, goals, etc. It is quite a juggling act, but it is necessary to live a fulfilling life.

It is easy to use the excuse that we just simply do not have enough time. That is a fallacy. We have the same twenty-four hours a day that Gandhi, Mother Teresa, and Thomas Edison had. The difference between us and them is that they knew how to properly prioritize. Prioritize your time by deciding what items are important or crucial.

To properly utilize your time, you must identify your time-wasters and learn how to overcome them. These are the activities that squander our time and are not productive. This could include watching TV or surfing the internet. Make a journal to assess how you spend your time for a week. Write down every activity and how long you spend doing it. You may be surprised how much time you do squander. Was the time spent on certain activities important or crucial? If not, you may want to re-evaluate your choices.

Set Limits
Learn how to set limits. Always be punctual. You don't want to

waste someone's time by being late. Make sure that meetings begin and end on time. Setting a structure can help to make the meeting more timely and efficient. Think about what you want to get out of the meeting before it begins. If you are the one organizing the meeting, ask yourself if the meeting is even necessary. Meetings can eat up a lot of time, so if you are having a meeting for the sake of having a meeting, rethink how that time could be better spent.

Get out of the habit of constantly checking your email throughout the day. It can be a distraction. If we spend our time constantly checking and answering emails, we will not get anything else done. Choose a time of day, maybe first thing in the morning, to check and answer emails. Set a time limit for doing so. If you have a lot of emails, set aside one hour out of your day for that task. Set an alarm on your phone to let you know when you have hit the one hour mark and stick to that limit. Start with answering the most recent emails first. If you are backlogged, your first inclination will be to answer the oldest emails, but what happens is new emails keep popping up, and some are probably related to one of the older ones. If you attack the newest ones first, you will be surprised how quickly you will knock those emails out.

Turn off all electronics before bed. Looking at your phone or tablet as you are trying to get ready for bed is damaging. The blue light that electronics emit is counterproductive to your sleep. It halts your body's production of melatonin. If you are on your smartphone looking at Facebook and have trouble falling asleep, now you know part of the reason why.

When you are around other people, make a habit of putting your electronics away. If you are constantly checking your phone at the dinner table, you are not being in the moment with the real people that are right there with you. It is not only a distraction, but it is downright rude.

Clutter can be the enemy. It can be a huge distraction. Some of us use our disorganization as a reason to put off our goals. *"I will work on my goal once I get my house clean."* Then, do it! Create three piles: Keep, Give Away, and Throw Away. If you have not used it in six months and you don't see yourself using it in six more months, get rid of it. If you think it could be of use to someone else, give it away. There are tons of shelters and thrift stores that would welcome your donation. They may also be tax deductible. If it is broken, worn out, or torn, recycle or toss it. If you haven't patched up that hole by now, you aren't going to. Quit creating more unnecessary tasks for yourself. *"But I spent a lot of money on these clothes. I'll try to sell them on eBay or consign them."* You have just given yourself another job to do! Do you really want to take the time to sell stuff, which is taking away time from your goal, to make a few bucks? The time that you will have to dedicate to doing that is more than likely not worth the small amount of money that you will make.

Why put off until tomorrow what you can do today! Procrastination is a major Achilles heel for most people. If your task falls under the important or urgent category, do it now. Once it is finished, you will feel so good about yourself and feel motivated to finish another task. Procrastination is only a way of putting off your success.

Take a break! I know you may be thinking, "I can't take a break. I have too much to do." Work for an hour, and then take a break for fifteen minutes, if possible. You need to regroup and refuel to avoid getting burned out and overwhelmed. Also, set time aside for meditation. Even ten minutes of meditation can be effective. It gives your brain a break, which may allow you to properly put things into perspective. It will help you manage time, because it will give you more balance.

As Jack Torrance says in *The Shining*, "All work and no play makes Jack a dull boy." You have to put time aside to stop and smell the roses. It is important to take the time to unwind from the stresses of the day.

Try out a few of these tips to de-stress:
- Take time to be alone and evaluate.
- Simplify your life. (eliminate what is not necessary)
- Deep, slow breathing.
- Do something each day that brings you joy.
- It's okay to say no.
- Exercise.
- Do the task "right now" – "tomorrow" never comes.
- Notice nature. – (also people, music, etc.)
- Do one thing, focused, at a time.
- Stay in the Present.
- Take a walk in your neighborhood.
- Listen to your favorite music.
- Make a date night with your significant other.
- Be aware of the demands you put on yourself.
- Prioritize.
- Smile and laugh more.
- Stop and smell the roses.

Be Prepared

Preparation aids time management. If you are fumbling around trying to find materials, you are wasting time. Keep the items that you use on a regular basis close at hand, and put away the things that don't get as much use. Being properly prepared frees up that time. Having a system of organization helps in preparation. Having folders properly labeled will save you time when looking for a document. Make a folder for each project, that includes physical files, computer files, and email files. This will make it easier to locate what is needed and make your system more functional.

Trying to pick out what to wear can be a daunting task. We can end up unnecessarily wasting a lot of time over what should take a few seconds to do. To avoid this, pick out what you are going to wear the night before. You can do this right before you go to bed as you are doing your nightly routines of brushing your teeth and washing your face. Have them ready and laying on a chair or hanging on the door.

Spend the last ten minutes of your workday making a list of what you need to accomplish the following day. Have it sitting on your desk waiting for you. It is easier for me to think of what needs to be done the night before. If I wait until the next morning, I am busy waking up or can't remember what I said that I had wanted to do. Prepare by doing it the night before, and make sure that you look at it the next day. A list means nothing if you do not use it.

Prioritizing

Not all tasks carry the same weight. Some tasks have a higher priority than others. You have to look at your list of tasks and determine which ones are important, urgent, or neither. Mailing a package so that it arrives for a meeting in time is urgent. Making a yearly doctor's appointment is important. Watching a recording on your DVR that you have already seen twice is neither important nor urgent.

Sometimes you can free some time up for yourself by delegating tasks to other people. Do you have someone that you work with that you could trust to do this task? When I was a manager, I felt compelled to try to do everything myself. I was a bit of a perfectionist. I wasn't sure if someone else would do it as well as I wanted it done, so I took on a lot of unnecessary workload. I had to learn to delegate to others. After all, if I trained them, I should be able to trust them to do the job. It makes them a stronger and valued employee, gives them a sense of purpose, and lightens your load.

Make a schedule. Block off time to work on projects. This provides structure to keep one on track to meet deadlines. If the goal you want to set is important, you must make time for it. In your schedule, block off what task you want to work on to complete your goal. Get a daily planner that has hourly designations. This will also show you where you are spending your time.

Organization In The Office

Your environment can dictate how you feel. If your space is cluttered and chaotic, you may feel more stressed and frazzled. An environment that is more welcoming will put your mental and emotional state more at ease. This is true for your office as well as your home.

Start by organizing your desk. It does not have to be clinical and barren. Have a picture of your loved one or a nice plant on your desk. Avoid a clock on your desk, because you will constantly be stopping what you are doing and checking the time. Put the clutter away; a place for everything, and everything in its place. If your space is littered with clutter, you may spend more time than desired looking for things. Instead of having loose papers piled up everywhere, develop a filing system with everything properly labeled. If you are worried about taking up room, a small, two-drawer filing cabinet can fit under your desk. Make sure your office supplies are close at hand and well stocked. You do not want to be in the middle of a project just to stop and look for paperclips and staples.

Display a basket or tray for incoming things that need attention. Another system could be two trays/baskets with one area for new and unopened documents and a second area for older pieces that you may have looked at but need attention. This will help to curb and eliminate paper clutter. Make sure that there is a wastebasket next to the desk. If you find that your wastebasket gets filled up quickly, replace it with a bigger one.

Plastic totes can be utilized for bigger items that need a place. If you have things that you use seasonally, place them in a labeled tote and store them for later. Making sure that things are properly labeled saves time from rifling through each tote to find something. Put smaller things like staplers and tape dispensers in a drawer or tray. This also clears up space on your desk.

"An ounce of performance is worth pounds of promises." ~ Mae West

In Conclusion

To find happiness, you must figure out what is your purpose. To discover your purpose, you must figure out what is important to you and what your values are. Once you uncover this, you must make out a plan and take action. Along with all of this, you must incorporate stress reduction techniques to keep you focused and avoid becoming overwhelmed.

Now go be happy!

REFERENCES/FURTHER READING

Music and the Brain: The Fascinating Ways That Music Affects Your Mood and Mind – By Barry Goldstein

Practical Intelligence: the Art & Science of Common Sense – by Karl Albrecht

Tao Te Ching

Chuang Tzu

The Tao of Pooh – Benjamin Hoff

The Te of Piglet – Benjamin Hoff

www.ingramcontent.com/pod-product-compliance
Lightning Source LLC
Chambersburg PA
CBHW032010170526
45157CB00002B/638